D0317044

Electronic Commerce
Opportunities and Challenges for Government

CITY OF WE̶   ̶TER
RECE̶

2 5 JUN 1997

WESTMINSTER REFERENCE LIBRARY

ORGANISATION FOR ECONOMIC CO-OPERATION AND DEVELOPMENT

ORGANISATION FOR ECONOMIC CO-OPERATION AND DEVELOPMENT

Pursuant to Article 1 of the Convention signed in Paris on 14th December 1960, and which came into force on 30th September 1961, the Organisation for Economic Co-operation and Development (OECD) shall promote policies designed:

- to achieve the highest sustainable economic growth and employment and a rising standard of living in Member countries, while maintaining financial stability, and thus to contribute to the development of the world economy;
- to contribute to sound economic expansion in Member as well as non-member countries in the process of economic development; and
- to contribute to the expansion of world trade on a multilateral, non-discriminatory basis in accordance with international obligations.

The original Member countries of the OECD are Austria, Belgium, Canada, Denmark, France, Germany, Greece, Iceland, Ireland, Italy, Luxembourg, the Netherlands, Norway, Portugal, Spain, Sweden, Switzerland, Turkey, the United Kingdom and the United States. The following countries became Members subsequently through accession at the dates indicated hereafter: Japan (28th April 1964), Finland (28th January 1969), Australia (7th June 1971), New Zealand (29th May 1973), Mexico (18th May 1994), the Czech Republic (21st December 1995), Hungary (7th May 1996), Poland (22nd November 1996) and the Republic of Korea (12th December 1996). The Commission of the European Communities takes part in the work of the OECD (Article 13 of the OECD Convention).

Publié en français sous le titre :

LE COMMERCE ÉLECTRONIQUE
Opportunités et défis pour les gouvernements

380 · 10285

WRF

© OECD 1997
Applications for permission to reproduce or translate all or part of this publication should be made to:
Head of Publications Service, OECD
2, rue André-Pascal, 75775 PARIS CEDEX 16, France.

380·10285

CITY OF WESTMINSTER
RECEIVED ON

2 5 JUN 1997

WESTMINSTER REFERENCE LIBRARY

PREFACE BY THE SECRETARY-GENERAL OF THE OECD

Our generation stands on the very cusp of the greatest technological revolution that mankind has ever faced. Some compare this age of electronic communication with the arrival of the Gutenberg press, or with the industrial revolution. Yet this revolution when it has run its course may have a greater impact on the planet than anything that has preceded. The applications of electronic transmissions are just beginning to be felt... and the breadth and depth of what lies ahead is only beginning to be fathomed. How and where we are educated, where and how we work and live, our health care systems, our shops, our commerce, our reading, our leisure... no part of human enterprise will be spared. Even our notions of sovereignty and governance could be profoundly affected.

Obviously the report of the Sacher Group is not intended to address this galaxy of realities and speculations. But it is a very significant step in the examination of these issues for three reasons.

First, it is a pioneering effort to assess these changes comprehensively in the context of increasing use of electronic networks for trade between firms and between firms and end-customers.

Second, it sets out the views of senior executives of major enterprises that are leading international users of electronic commerce. In addition, more than 100 high-level decision makers in firms and organisations that have emerged as important actors in this development were consulted by the Group. This background lends weight to the Report when it outlines what might be the strategic requirements of the new global electronic market-place.

Third, it suggests an agenda for government action. Electronic commerce should remain market-driven so that many of today's difficult problems can be overcome through the competitive interplay of market forces. However, the Report underlines the responsibilities of governments in providing appropriate regulatory frameworks while adapting their own administrative procedures and processes to remain tuned to the new developments.

The stakes are very high. The emergence of the electronic market-place holds the promise of renewed economic growth, expanded opportunities for consumers, new commercial activities, and new jobs. The report that follows provides inputs and insights that will be broadly discussed within the OECD, and will thus be a valuable contribution to the ongoing exploration of policy options.

A new partnership between governments and business has become a requirement in almost all sectors in the search for realistic solutions that will take full account of the diverse interests concerned. The Report demonstrates the potential value of such a dialogue which the OECD will continue to pursue with the business community and other groups in society.

In the name of the Organisation, I wish to express warm thanks to the members of the Ad Hoc Group of High-level Private Sector Experts on Electronic Commerce, and to their able Chairman John Sacher, who have devoted much effort to make this report possible. Their independent contribution helps us understand what may be the crucial economic issue of the 21st century, assess its implications, and progress towards a consensus among OECD Member countries on action needed to meet unprecedented challenges.

Donald J. Johnston

GROUP OF HIGH-LEVEL PRIVATE SECTOR EXPERTS ON ELECTRONIC COMMERCE

Mr. John SACHER (Chairman)
Executive Director
Marks and Spencer Plc

Mr. Roger ALEXANDER
Managing Director
Emerging Markets Unit
Barclays Bank PLC

Mr. Michael BEHRENS
Director, Information Organisation
Bertelsmann

Mr. Keith W BURROWES
Vice President and Manager
Information Systems and Services
Bechtel Corporation

Mr. Lloyd F. DARLINGTON
Executive Vice Chairman
Bank of Montréal

Mr. Jean Claude DISPAUX
Senior Vice President
Group IT and Logistics, Nestlé

Dr. Lutz EBERHARD
Head of Division TEI
Information Technology/Management
Daimler-Benz AG

Mr. Michael FISHER
Director
Bass Brewers Ltd.

Dr. Gunter FRANK
General Manager of Organisation
Dresdner Bank AG

Ms Cinda HALLMAN
Vice President
Information Systems
E. I. du Pont de Nemours & Company

Mr. Newt HARDIE
Vice President, Financial Planning
Milliken & Company

Mr. Allen Z. LOREN
Executive Vice President CIO
American Express Company

Mr. Andy MACDONALD
Chief Government Information Officer
Commonwealth of Australia

Mr. Randall MOTT
Senior Vice President and CIO
Corporate Information Systems
Wal-Mart Stores, Inc.

Mr. Atsushi NIIMURA
Managing Director
JCB CO. LTD

Mr Esa NORHOMAA
CEO
Aldata

Mr. Martin A STEIN
Vice Chairman
BankAmerica Corporation

Mr. Philippe TASSIN
Directeur Informatique et Télécommunication
Manufacture des Pneumatiques, Michelin

Mr. François VUILLEUMIER
Conseiller
Direction Générale des Douanes

SECRETARIAT

Mr. Georges FERNE
Principal Administrator
STP Division
OECD

Prof. Richard HAWKINS
SPRU University of Sussex

Mr. Jiro KOKURYO
Associate Professor
Graduate School of Business Administration
Keio University

TABLE OF CONTENTS

MAIN POINTS

Electronic Commerce refers generally to all forms of transactions relating to commercial activities, involving both organisations and individuals, that are based upon the processing and transmission of digitised data, including text, sound and visual images. It also refers to the effects that the electronic exchange of commercial information may have on the institutions and processes that support and govern commercial activities.

Firms engage in Electronic Commerce in order to achieve better management of commercial transactions and transaction-generated information, and to increase business efficiency. In today's globalising economic environment, however, the most important incentive is the opportunity to create whole new business areas for information and knowledge-based "intangible" products.

Although most current use of Electronic Commerce occurs at the inter-corporate and inter-organisational levels, Electronic Commerce services aimed at individual consumers are developing rapidly. The Internet is a major catalyst in the diffusion of Electronic Commerce into an increasing number of economic spheres, and is rapidly harmonizing the general environment in which electronic transactions of all kinds take place.

In order to foster confidence and trust in Electronic Commerce such that new opportunities can be exploited to maximise economic and social benefit, many issues must be addressed by both government and business. Governments must act in concert with each other, and with private sector users and suppliers of Electronic Commerce facilities, to create a commercial environment that is responsive to technical change.

Matters of particular importance are consumer protection and confidence, competition, financial and payment systems, taxation, intellectual property rights, security, legal safeguards against criminal activities, dispute settlement mechanisms as well as other emerging requirements that will stem from the regulation and development of the electronic and non-electronic infrastructures, and the social and cultural implications of Electronic Commerce.

Government and industry agendas with respect to Electronic Commerce are closely linked. As very large customers, and distributors of public services, governments have much to gain from the application of Electronic Administration principles, which are evolving symbiotically with Electronic Commerce.

Electronic Commerce is part of an evolving approach to business and administration that could eventually involve the application of information and communication technologies to an enormous range of production and distribution processes on a global scale. Although many characteristics of Electronic Commerce are only beginning to become clear, the Group expects that it will grow very quickly and that its effects on society as a whole will be dramatic. As a matter of urgency, therefore, public and private sector institutions must re-evaluate many of the economic, legal and political frameworks that currently govern commercial activities and the technological and social environments in which they take place.

POLICY RECOMMENDATIONS

In order that quickly developing opportunities in Electronic Commerce can be grasped creatively, efficiently and productively, the High-Level Group considers that there are three priority areas for government action.

(1) Supporting opportunities for the growth of Electronic Commerce

(a) *Regulation of the information infrastructure*

Electronic services infrastructures like telecommunications, television and data networking, as well as the regulatory regimes that effect them, must be permitted and encouraged to converge in order to reflect the rapid convergence of networking technologies employed in Electronic Commerce applications.

While improvements to infrastructure provision for corporate to corporate business are beginning to take place, little has happened that will benefit the individual consumer. There are insufficient market-generated infrastructure improvements being developed internationally. Where substantial progress is not being made it may be necessary through the regulatory environment to encourage the development of managed network facilities for Electronic Commerce – particularly through managed Internet facilities – that can respond flexibly to the needs of a growing diversity of commercial users. Governments should evaluate current competition policies to ensure that they do not impede orderly development of the information and communication infrastructure.

(b) *Standardization*

Although in many cases non-proprietary standards are the preferred solution for Electronic Commerce applications, the rapid pace of technological and business development almost certainly will outstrip the ability of standards organisations to respond to market needs in a timely manner. The Group urges governments to adopt a pragmatic approach that does not discourage the development of widely accepted proprietary solutions becoming adopted as if they were standards for Electronic Commerce, but which nevertheless monitors standardization developments closely to ensure that proprietary standards do not become barriers to market entry or impediments to further innovation.

(c)   Information exchange

While recognising the legitimate security and law enforcement responsibilities of governments, it is essential that they be prepared to accept multiple solutions to encryption problems. No country should be able to enforce national encryption policies on firms in other countries as a condition of market entry, and encryption policies should not be adopted that operate to the disadvantage of the honest trader. The Group broadly supports the ongoing efforts of the OECD, in consultation with the private sector, to negotiate international guidelines for the development and use of cryptography, and for determining the criteria for legal access to encrypted data.

National data protection laws should be harmonized early in order to prevent situations that could destroy public confidence in Electronic Commerce where privacy and confidentiality implications are concerned. Harmonization should not, however, be promoted in a way that would inhibit the legitimate use of databases. Governments should not act to restrict transborder data flows unduly, but should act multilaterally to minimise the possibility of abuse in the utilisation of customer information when databases are transported from one jurisdiction to another.

(d)   The "physical" infrastructure

Where Electronic Commerce is applied to the production and distribution of tangible goods, a close relationship exists between the electronic and the non-electronic components of the commercial infrastructure. Electronic Commerce cannot function on its own. Costly and inefficient systems for the physical transportation of goods could slow down the development of the electronic market-place. Governments have a major role to play in ensuring that physical transportation infrastructures are developed in coherent, co-ordinated ways, such that they complement the transaction efficiencies generated by Electronic Commerce and do not interfere with speedy process.

(e)   Development of high-level action plans that reflect the pace of technical change

In order to ensure close communication with industry, governments should give early consideration to the development of high-level statements outlining proposed actions of relevance to Electronic Commerce, along with time scales.

(2)   Raising the visibility of Electronic Commerce, and promoting productive industry/government relations

(a)   Co-ordinating public and private sector Electronic Commerce activities

To ensure the productive co-ordination of public and private sector agendas for the application of Electronic Commerce, every government should have a Chief Information Officer, or some other highly visible single locus of activity for national information and communication activities. In general, all government actions in areas of importance to Electronic Commerce should be given high visibility in order to generate and sustain public confidence and trust in the emerging Electronic Commerce environment.

(b)   Ensuring flexibility in public/private sector relationships

Industry and government should maintain a dynamic international dialogue on the harmonization of Electronic Commerce and Electronic Administration principles. Public sector practices must be made responsive to the substantial changes in the business environment that are expected to occur with the diffusion of Electronic Commerce. This applies particularly to procurement practices, and to all administrative reporting procedures that are required of industry by governments.

(c)   Awareness, education and skills

Governments should promote awareness of the potential of Electronic Commerce in all sectors of the economy, and, in consultation with industry, work to reflect the rapidly changing professional and skills requirements of the electronic market-place in education, training and employment programmes.

(3) Defining new principles for the governance of economic activity in an electronic environment

(a) Reforming regulatory practices

Government support for the concept of liberalised electronic services markets must be backed up with real changes in regulatory practices. Badly conceived de-regulation and re-regulation can provide new forms of protection to existing monopolies, and can be worse than preserving the *status quo*.

New kinds of regulation may be required to prevent new infrastructure providers from acquiring market power on a scale equivalent to that exercised by incumbent infrastructure monopolies, but new regulation must not prevent better infrastructure management.

(b) Clarification and revision of laws and regulations

As a matter of urgency, governments need to clarify the legal definitions, practices and structures that pertain to commercial activities in an electronic environment, and to seek multilateral agreements on critical legal matters, especially the laws regarding residency, agency, liability, auditability, control of databases, unauthorised use of databases and data protection.

Where appropriate, governments should adjust existing laws and regulations so that they apply to "intangible" as well as "material" product environments. They should ensure that all future actions regarding consumer protection laws and regulations are closely co-ordinated with developments in Electronic Commerce.

Recognising the special characteristics of the commercial environment provided by the Internet, an internationally agreed legal definition is urgently required as to where commercial transactions on the Internet are deemed to have taken place.

(c) Enforcement of laws

An internationally clarified legal environment must be supported by international agreement on policing and enforcement.

(d)   ***Protection of intellectual property***

The scope, nature and international coherence of IPR systems must be reviewed in light of emerging Electronic Commerce requirements. We urge the OECD to undertake such an assessment in co-operation with the other international organisations concerned, in particular the World Trade Organisation and the World Intellectual Property Organisation.

(e)   ***Taxation***

As a matter of principle, the Group opposes proposals that are oriented to taxing the process of data exchange (the "bit tax"), as unworkable and potentially discriminatory to Electronic Commerce activities and to normal business communications. The Group supports approaches to taxation based on principles relating to the source and destination of products, be they tangible or intangible, and of residency of companies.

REPORT

The *aim* of this Report is to provide a foundation for productive dialogue between business and government, based on a synthesis of the collected experience of a group of significant participants in the development of Electronic Commerce. Many of these participants speak from long experience with successive generations of commercial networking systems. Others are still exploring the possibilities of Electronic Commerce. Some have more immediate incentives than others to be proactive in developing this new environment. All believe strongly in the potential of Electronic Commerce, and in the necessity to allow this new tool to develop freely in response to evolving business conditions.

The Report is based substantially on information provided directly to the Secretariat by members of the Group, much of it gathered through direct contact between Group members and nearly 100 individuals in more than eighty firms and organisations around the world that are currently playing major roles in the development of Electronic Commerce. The Report presents a synthesis of this information. Although the Group was made up primarily of users, the firms and organisations consulted represented a very wide spectrum of "supplier" interests, including computer equipment vendors, telecommunication companies, network services providers, software houses and public sector agencies. (A list of the firms and organisations consulted is provided in Annex B.)

The Report has three main objectives.

◊ to define and describe Electronic Commerce and to assess its immediate and longer-term potential;

◊ to outline the main opportunities and issues affecting the future development of Electronic Commerce;

◊ to discuss the implications of Electronic Commerce for governments.

I.   Defining Electronic Commerce and Assessing its Potential

Electronic Commerce refers generally to all forms of commercial transactions involving both organisations and individuals, that are based upon the electronic processing and transmission of data, including text, sound and visual images. It also refers to the effects that the electronic exchange of commercial information may have on the institutions and processes that support and govern commercial activities. These include organisational management, commercial negotiations and contracts, legal and regulatory frameworks, financial settlement arrangements, and taxation, among many others.

Electronic Commerce is part of an evolving approach to business that could eventually involve the application of information and communication technologies (ICT) to the production and distribution of goods and services on a global scale. Some elements of Electronic Commerce are "non-transactional" – geared to the provision of information about products and services, the delivery of information-based ("intangible") products to customers, and the support of supply chains. The completed process, however, is "transactional" – geared directly to processes of trade in goods and services.

Electronic Commerce can be used to support fully automated transactions, but, for the immediate future at least, it also encompasses many partially automated transactions involving human and physical interfaces and intermediaries of various kinds. In some circumstances, telephones, fax machines, and face-to-face contact can be as much a part of an Electronic Commerce transaction as computers and broadband data networks. Moreover, many non-transactional Electronic Commerce elements – catalogues, advertising and so forth – are oriented towards an eventual face-to-face transaction. Furthermore, Electronic Commerce interacts not only with electronic distribution systems, as in electronic publishing or financial services applications, but also with the physical infrastructure for the distribution of manufactured products.

Electronic Commerce can occur within and between three basic participant groups – business, government, and individuals (see Figure 1). At present, and by a large margin, most Electronic Commerce occurs on a business-to-business level, although substantial activity also occurs at a business-to-government level in connection with public procurement, and with administrative functions like customs and excise. This will change significantly as Electronic

Commerce facilities become more widely available – particularly to individuals. Currently, Electronic Commerce at the business-to-individual and individual-to-individual levels, and at the government-to-individual level in the delivery of government services, occurs on a comparatively small scale. Nevertheless, the members of the Group fully expect that Electronic Commerce centred on the individual will assume a position of major economic importance in the near future, and that the consequences will be dramatic for business endeavours of all kinds.

Figure 1. **Participant Groups in Electronic Commerce**

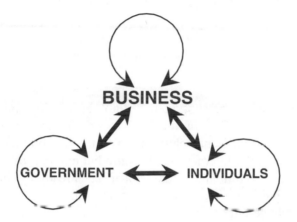

Source: Diagram developed by J. Kokuryo, Graduate School of Business Administration, Keio University, Yokohama.

The idea of the "electronic market-place" is certainly not new, but past activity involving electronic transactions has tended to occur in discrete industrial or product clusters, normally centred around a significant organisation, such as a leading firm, or government agency.   The use of ICT to provide a direct, general interface between a wide range of customers and a wide range of products is a more recent development, spurred on in large part by the diffusion of data networking systems, and, in particular, by the tremendous recent growth in the Internet in corporate as well as individual contexts.

Electronic Commerce sets up two related tensions in the market-place. First, even though much electronic business will continue to be transacted in domestic markets, Electronic Commerce is difficult to contain within geographically defined trade areas and frontier-based regulatory and administrative regimes.   As electronic network facilities increase in sophistication they tend to become oriented to an international trading context. Electronic Commerce facilitates the globalisation of business by providing more economical access to distant markets, and by supporting new opportunities for firms to increase economies of scale and scope by distributing their production and distribution assets internationally.

The second tension concerns the "intangible" nature of many goods and services in an Electronic Commerce environment. For non-electronic transactions in a "material" product environment, the source of a product, the locations of its suppliers and distributors, and the respective responsibilities and liabilities of the buyer and seller can be verified relatively easily. On the other hand, intangible transactions blur many of the existing distinctions between domestic and foreign business, and between on-shore and off-shore transactions. Indeed, probably the most troublesome conceptual aspect of Electronic Commerce is that it can be very difficult to define the location at which a transaction actually takes place, and hence the jurisdictions to which it may be subject.

Electronic Commerce can be supported technologically in a number of ways, but it is the considered view of the High-Level Group that the Internet is potentially the most significant vehicle for Electronic Commerce to have yet emerged. Ultimately, the Internet may become but one part of a much broader evolution in electronic communications, but it has already established the first basic networking paradigm that could eventually allow Electronic Commerce facilities to be extended throughout the entire spectrum of commercial activity. An important aspect of Internet evolution for Electronic Commerce purposes will be the development of managed network facilities to bridge the gap that currently exists between the largely unmanaged public Internet domain, and the rapid proliferation of private corporate Internets. Another important aspect will be the rapidly increasing convergence between the various computer, telecommunication and broadcast media that are or could be used to provide mass Internet access.

Many believe that we are entering the era of the virtual enterprise in which maximum flexibility in the organisational and even physical distribution of business resources is facilitated by ICT. Irrespective of how "virtual" these enterprises actually become, however, Electronic Commerce promises many immediate practical advantages for firms as they face an increasingly globalised market-place. Much evidence is accumulating that Electronic Commerce applications can contribute to increased responsiveness, flexibility, efficiency and accountability in business structures. Moreover, many of the most promising new business areas are intangible in nature – defined by the exchange of information and knowledge, rather than by the exchange of physical objects. Increased business efficiency, coupled with the development of new kinds of products and markets, has many positive implications for the health of the economy as a whole.

At this point in time, developments in Electronic Commerce are particularly dynamic. Electronic Commerce takes many forms, stems from many incentives, incorporates a wide spectrum of technologies, and is applied in diverse ways to many different types of products and markets. Tele-shopping, home banking and on-line information services are facets of Electronic Commerce, but so is corporate and inter-corporate supply-chain management. Likewise, Electronic Commerce activities can be supported by many kinds of networking environments, but no single network technology or configuration of technologies constitutes Electronic Commerce in itself.

Electronic Commerce is more than an accumulation of ICT applications related to miscellaneous business processes. In the broadest sense, the goal of Electronic Commerce is the creation of a new kind of commercial environment in an electronic milieu. Indications are beginning to emerge as to how Electronic Commerce might evolve, but many questions remain. These include the long-term impacts of Electronic Commerce on competition and competitiveness, the effects on prices, the influence on enterprise mobility, the effects on consumer behaviour, and the implications for the institutional structures that govern and facilitate commercial activities. The effects of Electronic Commerce on the workplace seem likely to be particularly profound as it will induce significant changes in the ways work is defined and managed. In general terms, the role of ICT in job creation and productivity is only beginning to be understood. Electronic Commerce may create many new employment opportunities, but it may also facilitate the international mobility of enterprises.

What is certain is that Electronic Commerce is here to stay. Many major participants in the international market-place, and in government, are now actively pursuing enterprise development strategies centred around the increasingly sophisticated commercial capabilities of the ICT network infrastructure. The potential and the problems of Electronic Commerce are now becoming central to the agendas of business and governments alike. The Group believes that for Electronic Commerce to fulfil its economic and social potential, it is absolutely essential that these agendas do not conflict needlessly.

1. Realising the economic potential of Electronic Commerce

Electronic Commerce is a marriage between a rapidly evolving technical environment and an increasingly pervasive set of ideas as to how markets should function. However, markets involve complex interactions between specific business/organisational factors, and general economic, social and political factors. At this point in time, the full economic potential of Electronic Commerce can only be evaluated against a backdrop of rapid change on all of these fronts. Nevertheless, there are strong current indications that massive changes have already begun to occur across the entire business spectrum.

The effects of mature or maturing Electronic Commerce applications on many types of inter-corporate commercial relationships have been significant for some time. The Group received information from a major bank, for example, that it currently conducts some 10 million electronic transactions per day, and from another bank that about 70 per cent of its transactions are now automated. A major retailer reported that 100 per cent of its total annual transactions with suppliers, amounting to over US$10 billion, are now conducted electronically. A major European automobile manufacturer reported that it maintains electronic connections with over 800 suppliers, supporting transaction volumes of nearly US$7 billion per year, and a US aerospace firm reported that 60 per cent of orders for spare and replacement parts are fully automated, enabling delivery anywhere in the world in less than 24 hours. Members of the Group found statistics like these to be typical among many of the firms contacted.

In the inter-corporate environment, the potential significance of Electronic Commerce is often underrated by focusing too selectively on particular clusters of technologies and services. To give an example, Electronic Commerce is frequently, and erroneously, equated with Electronic Data Interchange (EDI), or regarded simply as an enhancement of EDI. Although it is certainly one of the core technologies that currently supports many kinds of Electronic Commerce, EDI is oriented specifically to the exchange of highly structured accounting and procurement data, thus limiting its use to specific kinds of transactions. In the European Union, for example, only about 40 000 firms were regular EDI users as of the beginning of 1995, although the user base is growing at ten to fifteen per cent per year.[1]

Similarly, there are difficulties in assessing the commercial potential of the Internet. The Internet is the first multifunctional digital information environment that is available to a wide spectrum of users, ranging from large organisations to individuals, and it will likely become a focal point for the convergence of access media and the development of interactive services.

24

Many believe that the Internet has the potential to become a basic vehicle for the delivery of virtually any kind of electronic service. Over the past few years, the advent of the World Wide Web (WWW) has spurred development of increasingly user-friendly navigational tools that allow all of the information resources on the Internet to be treated as a single comprehensive entity. Nevertheless, the problem remains that for most individual users the Internet is still too difficult to access and use. In all likelihood, however, this will be a short-term problem, as relatively simple television-based "set-top" access devices proliferate, and as the consumer-oriented products of computer hardware and software firms undergo further innovation.

The cited figures for the actual and projected growth of Internet connections and services are impressive, but their reliability and significance is often open to question. Estimates as to the current number of Internet users vary widely between about 30 million and 50 million, but these are difficult to verify. Probably a more reliable indicator is the growth in Internet hosts (the number of computers attached to the Internet). A recent OECD study determined that between 1991 and 1996, the number of hosts increased world-wide from just over half a million to just over nine million.[2]

Although growth in the Internet is not the same phenomenon as growth in Electronic Commerce, new vistas for Electronic Commerce are continually opening up on the Internet. In particular, the spectacular rates of increase in the numbers of households with Internet access has drawn special attention to prospects for direct sales to individual consumers. In this regard, companies are learning to identify the many new consumer communities that are emerging in the Internet environment, and to evaluate their product and service needs. Relatively mature communities have developed already around electronic services in the areas of travel and tourism, road navigation and health, for example.

Typical market projections for merchandising on the Internet predict growth from a present base of about US$500 million to US$5 billion and more by the year 2000. Irrespective of the accuracy of these projections, the claimed rates of growth for many existing "cyber-firms" are spectacular. Although Web-based firms have only existed since about 1994, it is estimated that there are now 250 000 of them in the United States alone. Moreover, a recent market research survey of 1 100 US Web-based firms suggested that over thirty per cent were profitable and that nearly thirty per cent more expected to be profitable within two years. Reported net profit margins of twenty per cent and above are common.[3] Consistent with the notion of developing new consumer communities, many (if not most) of the successful cyber-firms were those that exploited new market niches and merchandising concepts that were particularly suited to the capabilities of the Internet and the social profiles of particular groups of network users.

Although the reliability of surveys and projections like these is always open to question, it is the considered view of the Group that they are broadly indicative of actual trends – indeed, in some cases (media services for example), they may actually understate the growth potential. Nevertheless, by focusing too much attention on early attempts to provide Internet merchandising services, we risk overlooking the overall significance of the Internet for Electronic Commerce. The Internet has a corporate as well as a consumer face. Firms and organisations can construct a wide variety of communications capabilities behind protective "firewalls". A recent estimate is that the number of currently registered addresses for private Internets exceeds the number of public Internet addresses by nearly five-to-one.[4]

An increasing number of firms are using Web-sites to disseminate product information, or to facilitate product support and logistics processes with existing customers and suppliers. Current problems with speed, reliability and security are deterring firms from migrating to the Internet as their principal backbone communications facility, but increasing numbers of firms are shifting significant parts of their current communications profiles (like e-mail and some EDI applications) to the Internet.

Once again, however, the potential of Electronic Commerce cannot be assessed merely in terms of network growth. As many of the Group's correspondents were keen to stress, effective business planning for Electronic Commerce demands a detailed, medium- to long-term view. Particularly at the customer interface, it is not enough simply to react to Internet growth projections. It is necessary to assess how many real commercial users of the Internet there are likely to be several years hence, and to determine what kind of customers they will be in terms of the kinds of products that may become available.

A recent study of individual and corporate use of Web facilities revealed that exploration was the primary individual activity, and that information gathering was the primary corporate use. Nevertheless, 14 per cent of individual users and 23 per cent of corporate users reported that they had completed at least one commercial transaction on the Web.[5] Moreover, market research shows that some consumer products are more likely to be sought out and purchased in an on-line environment than others. Not surprisingly, computer software products top most lists of products ordered electronically. The electronic purchase of many other types of goods appears to be much more culturally determined, and electronic markets for different goods will likely grow at individual and uncertain rates. Most significantly, however, substantial numbers of consumers now make electronic purchases of information and entertainment products like books and Compact Disks, and service products like airline tickets – some of them products that could soon migrate entirely to an electronic format.

The huge capacity of facilities like the Internet requires the development of Electronic Commerce applications that allow buyers to locate products and information about products quickly and easily, and to conduct transactions in a simple and straightforward manner. However, navigating electronic networks, including the Internet, is still a complex task, and the learning curve on most software products is still too steep to encourage mass access. Netscape Navigator and Microsoft Explorer have shown the way forward, but they are still not intuitive enough for many potential users.

At this point in time, the electronic customer is not the typical customer. Electronic Commerce currently draws most of its consumer users from the ranks of those with experience of interactive computer applications in other contexts. Most adult users of Internet commerce facilities are likely to be educated to a higher than average level, relatively affluent, and familiar with computer use in the workplace. Clearly, expansion of this base will require matching the right kinds of products to the right kinds of network interfaces. Experience has shown that as more Electronic Commerce services become available to more users, they come to expect an increasing service range. Having successfully used Internet banking, for example, the user is likely to search for other kinds of electronic financial services, and to be more open to purchasing other types of products.

At this stage in the development of Electronic Commerce, many of the aspects of inter-corporate and consumer Electronic Commerce applications must be evaluated separately in terms of their economic potential. However, developments like the Internet are already bringing the consumer and corporate Electronic Commerce environments steadily together. The workplace (including schools and universities) is the most common source of computer awareness and skills that become transferred to the household.

The significance and growth potential of Electronic Commerce is linked interactively to the broader socialisation of the electronic networking environment, a phenomenon that looks certain to proliferate with each generation. Indeed, evidence for this is already accumulating. Recent figures provided to the Group by a major on-line services provider indicated that subscribers in one or two countries already spend more time per week accessing on-line services than other kinds of electronic and non-electronic media, and that the average number of on-line hours per week, per subscriber, has doubled within six months.

2. *Incentives for engaging in Electronic Commerce*

The economic potential of Electronic Commerce is significant, but the pace and patterns of its diffusion are likely to be diverse. In their consultations with firms, members of the High-Level group noted many differences in the propensity of firms to engage in Electronic Commerce, and in the types of transactions most likely to lead their migration into an Electronic Commerce environment. Much was found to depend on the kind of industry and product involved, and, most importantly, on the type of customer-supplier relationship that it was necessary either to preserve, or to develop.

Electronic Commerce will not emerge all at once in a standardized form, and it will progress differently according to the requirements of particular industries. Nevertheless, there are certain common incentives for engaging with Electronic Commerce that transcend corporate and sector boundaries.

(a) *Transaction management*

In Electronic Commerce, many of the separate steps that normally intervene between a buyer and a seller in a commercial transaction can be integrated and automated electronically. For example, the steps in a typical non-electronic purchasing transaction may include locating products and evaluating their characteristics, comparing and/or negotiating prices, ordering and invoicing, making payment, and arranging terms of delivery. Moreover, many of these steps can involve various forms of intermediation by third parties. Each step in a transaction involves an exchange of information that incurs costs. Historically, these costs have tended to increase as a function of time and distance.

Electronic networking minimises many of the economic impacts of time and distance. In an electronic environment, moreover, commercial transactions are just as likely to relate to intangible products and services, as they are to tangible products. The promise of Electronic Commerce is that transaction costs can be constrained to the minimum that is appropriate to each type of transaction. Fulfilling this promise, however, is not just a technological problem. A wide range of complementary conditions is required to transpose existing market relationships into an electronic market-place, and to allow new kinds of market relationships to evolve. These will involve institutional adjustments, and new approaches to organisational and inter-organisational management.

Irrespective of expected savings in transaction costs, one of the most important incentives for firms to engage in Electronic Commerce is the need for more efficient transaction management. At the most basic level, the need is to respond to the escalating quantity and complexity of transactions. In the travel sector, for example, major carriers are examining closely the possibility of migrating to electronic ticketing systems. In Europe, electronic linkages are being planned between rail and airline reservation systems.

At another level, there is the need to cope with escalation in the generation of transaction-associated data. This is especially critical where complex, interactive logistical arrangements must be maintained. In paper form, for example, the documentation for many kinds of complex technological systems can run into millions of printed pages. Distributing this information electronically not only facilitates more efficient storage and retrieval, but also helps ensure that operators of these systems always access the most up-to-date manuals, thus increasing their margins of safety and reliability. Throughout industry, not only is the amount of transaction-related data increasing, but the awareness of the potential value of this data is increasing also.

(b)   Business efficiency

Another major incentive is the desire to achieve greater production and distribution efficiencies. All contemporary production methodologies are dependent upon highly dynamic information flows in supply chains. Firms deploy ICT as part of programmes to support and/or promote organisational and process change in order better to meet the challenges of what they see as an increasingly global business environment.

Electronic Commerce supports advanced design and manufacturing concepts like Just-in-Time, Quick Response, and Concurrent Engineering, all oriented to co-ordinating and often integrating various aspects of the production and distribution processes. Electronic Commerce also facilitates new kinds of on-demand marketing concepts throughout a wide range of products. Levi-Strauss now uses electronic links with retailers to supply made-to-measure clothing, for example, and several automotive manufacturers now virtually assemble cars to order according to specifications worked out between the customer and the dealer.

The ways in which Electronic Commerce is employed to achieve business efficiency goals vary according to the types of business processes involved. For manufacturers of airliners, most existing Electronic Commerce applications are downstream with airlines, rather than upstream with component suppliers. This reflects the extensive logistics and maintenance requirements inherent to this industry. Nevertheless, the general trend noted by most of the manufacturing firms contacted by the Group is that there has been substantial recent growth in the amount of data shared electronically between design and tool-making teams on an intra- and inter-firm basis. This is reflective of the increasing amount of enterprise integration in the design and production of components.

By contrast, electronic links are deployed in the insurance industry more to link remote operatives to home offices, than to link customers to firms. In this industry, it is the insurer who decides to do business with the customer and not the other way around (*i.e.* the insurer must decide whether or not to accept the risk). Insurers have few routine transactions with customers, and most insurance claims processing is not electronic. Banks, on the other hand, must cope with huge numbers of routine transactions, and, historically, have been in the forefront of data communications, both internally and with customers.

Electronic Commerce generates transaction information that can be captured and archived immediately in a form that permits sophisticated processing and quick distribution. This information can then be used to assess market conditions, but it can also be used to plan and support changes designed to increase the responsiveness, flexibility, efficiency and accountability of business processes.

In this respect, the development and creative use of customer information databases has assumed greatly increased importance in the operations and strategies of firms. In the insurance industry, Electronic Commerce is being used dynamically with corporate customers in a risk management role. Closer to the consumer interface, large retail traders use electronically gathered information on consumer buying patterns – often involving the use of "affinity" or "loyalty" cards – to assist them in targeting products efficiently to specific kinds of customers. As the need to expand the use of customer databases increases, however, many new security, privacy and legal issues arise that will require concerted action by business and governments.

(c)   New market development

In the past, many firms have become involved in electronic business relationships for reactive or even negative reasons. It is estimated, for example, that up to 70 per cent of EDI links are established by firms primarily because a major corporate or government customer specifies this requirement as a term of contract.[6] Other firms have adopted ICT in a "bandwagon" scenario – simply reacting to ICT deployment by competitors.

Increasingly, however, many firms are taking a more positive and proactive stance. As firms perceive Electronic Commerce less in terms of mere automation, and more in terms of creating business opportunities, they learn to apply ICT to business processes in order to position themselves strategically with respect to new market opportunities. Indeed, in an increasing number of industries, Electronic Commerce has already become firmly established as a standard business tool, thus moving beyond cost saving and strategic objectives altogether.

Probably the most significant incentive for Electronic Commerce is new market development. This involves extending existing Electronic Commerce practices and infrastructure into new market areas. Thus, Electronic Commerce links set up initially on an inter-firm basis (as between manufacturers and financial institutions, for example) soon develop interfaces with a greater variety of uses and users. Likewise, Electronic Commerce links established in one sector (shipping and forwarding, for example) can migrate into other sectors (like retailing and manufacturing).

At a more mature level, the nature of the original business can expand, and new types of business can substitute for others in economic importance, particularly where it becomes possible to exploit the commercial potential of intangible products. In the transport industry, intangible support services like dispatch, routing and reservation systems are being developed into products in their own right, thus creating major new revenue producing business areas. Many highly visible new markets for intangible products are being created around changing patterns of work and leisure – allowing consumers to access such services as banking, insurance and travel reservations directly from their own homes and businesses, both in and out of normal office hours. Likewise, new markets are being developed by the purveyors of information and entertainment services as media converge and become more interactive. Electronic newspapers, for example, can now link readers directly to the firms that advertise in these publications.

Services like these can employ a variety of access media – including personal computers (PCs), videotext terminals, and interactive television – but their impact is not necessarily related to the technical sophistication of the customer interface. In only a few years, direct sale by telephone has become the principal method for marketing automobile insurance in the United Kingdom, and, for the present at least, the ordinary credit card is proving to be acceptable to many consumers as a payment mechanism.

One of the potentially most important areas of business development in an Electronic Commerce environment is education and training. Of particular importance is the reciprocal nature of this activity. Not only is it rapidly becoming a business area in its own right, but it is a major contributor to building up the infrastructure of skills upon which new generations of electronic services markets will develop.

II.   The Mechanics of Electronic Commerce

1.   *The business dimensions of Electronic Commerce*

Commercial transactions can be carried out between vendors of goods or services and final customers, and between the various entities that interact in the supply and production chains that result in finished goods. The latter type of transaction may be invisible to the final customer, but it is a very significant economic activity. The greatest amount of trade world-wide occurs between firms engaged in supply chains, and the majority of electronic transactions are carried out in intra-firm and inter-firm contexts.

Accordingly, there are two basic and interactive business dimensions to Electronic Commerce:

> *(i) The customer dimension* – This refers to the placing of finished goods and services with final customers. These customers can be corporate entities or individual consumers. Where tangible goods are concerned, the primary function of the electronic infrastructure is to provide catalogue, ordering, billing, payment and dispatch facilities. Tangible goods must be delivered using physical infrastructures. Where intangible products are involved, every element in the transaction is normally electronic, including distribution.

(ii)The enterprise dimension – This has primarily an inter-corporate or inter-organisational (including business-to-government) supply chain orientation, with the final objective of achieving flexibility and efficiency gains in design, procurement, manufacturing and logistics processes related to the production of components, their assembly into finished products, and their delivery to the final point of sale. In some cases, this dimension can also encompass product support and maintenance.

The relationship between these business dimensions is continuous and complex. Indeed, in many cases, it is difficult to draw a distinction between the two, especially where intangible products are involved, as a single firm can be involved in both dimensions. Some manufacturers bypass the distribution chain altogether by selling direct to their final customers. Others sell both direct and through intermediaries. Some retail and wholesale firms are also manufacturers, or otherwise engaged directly in production supply chains in that they provide customised designs and product specifications to their suppliers.

In the business strategies of individual firms, these Electronic Commerce business dimensions will tend to be balanced according to the nature of the product or service concerned. Electronic publishers and financial services companies will be especially concerned to provide a high quality direct marketing interface with individual consumers. Manufacturers of commercial airliners, on the other hand, do not sell products directly to consumers. Their interest in Electronic Commerce will relate to co-ordinating logistics and maintenance functions with the airlines, and design, procurement and production functions with the suppliers of components and sub-assemblies.

Significantly, however, Electronic Commerce can also facilitate migration between the customer and enterprise dimensions. Thus, for example, automobile manufacturers who now use electronic networks primarily to support production and maintenance supply chains, and to communicate with franchised dealers, could eventually use Electronic Commerce to sell their products directly to individual consumers, perhaps employing virtual showrooms to illustrate various design options.

2.   *The technological dimensions of Electronic Commerce*

The technological dimensions of Electronic Commerce can be classified according to the three basic functions of any market environment:

(i) Access dimension – Electronic communication infrastructures are required to allow buyers and sellers to make and maintain contact with each other, and to facilitate the transfer of information about products and customer needs into the market-place. Information can be exchanged in structured formats (as with EDI systems), or in relatively unstructured and informal ways (as with telephone sales). Electronic Commerce makes extensive use of public telecommunication network facilities such as voice telephony, fax, audiotext, and teleconferencing. It also uses computer-based communication facilities over the public network, like data networking, e-mail, electronic bulletin boards, on-line databases and the Internet. Electronic Commerce can also employ broadcast and cable network services like interactive television and videotext. Particularly in enterprises, Electronic Commerce makes extensive use of private network technologies in local area networks (LAN) and wide area networks (WAN).

(ii)Transaction dimension – Specialised technologies are required to support specific kinds of structured information exchanges that are related directly to the setting up and completion of commercial transactions, and the performance of contractual obligations. Examples are EDI, electronic point-of-sale devices, credit, debit and smart cards, Automated Teller Machines, and electronic funds transfer.

(iii)Support dimension – Other specialised technologies are required to lend administrative and technical support to transactions carried out in the electronic market-place. This includes electronic archiving of product specifications and prices, certification of buyer and seller identities, credit checks, guarantees and address validation. Specific examples are credit card validation technologies, bar-coding devices, and electronic clearing and settlement mechanisms. EDI can be applied to support as well as to transaction functions.

Box 1. From Credit Card to Smart Card – Transition or Revolution?

The credit card was first introduced in the 1960s. It was the first widely available mechanism that allowed ordinary individuals to conduct "on-the-spot" guaranteed transactions involving deferred payment and credit. In effect, the credit card made it possible for the consumer to write his or her own loan. Card technology has undergone considerable evolution, and current applications include everything from the now ubiquitous credit card to advanced "smart-card" applications that could support a multiplicity of commercial and non-commercial functionalities.

The credit card was a revolutionary development and it has proven to be very adaptable to the requirements of Electronic Commerce at the consumer level. More questionable, however, is the future of card-based systems. Some believe that card technology will become the ubiquitous access medium for Electronic Commerce; others believe that cards are a transitional technology that will be supplanted eventually by new types of interactive "real-time" interfaces. At this point, however, it seems certain that various types of card-based technologies, existing or under development, will have a significant impact on the diffusion of Electronic Commerce – particularly for consumer transactions. The first generation of cards were primarily applied to payment functions, and required data entry and validation checks to be carried out manually. This process is being supplanted rapidly by electronic systems employing "personal identification numbers" (PIN) in conjunction with card-holder codes that are stored on the card itself, either on a magnetic stripe, or on an embedded computer chip – the "smart card". In either case, the customer's PIN must correspond to validation codes before a transaction is authorised. This automated validation procedure, whether self contained or not, began to enhance the value of the card as a general identification and authentication device.

In North America, cheap "dial-up" access to centralised databases for validation purposes initially rendered the smart card unnecessary and uneconomical. In Europe, however, where dial-up access was expensive, there were economic advantages in being able to minimise access to central databases by matching the PIN directly with information stored on the card. For Electronic Commerce purposes, smart cards offer certain advantages in that they can store more information than a magnetic stripe card, and they can be used to conduct more complex tasks involving interactions with various types of terminals. Smart cards also offer security advantages in that the computer code is embedded in hardware, thus making them much more "tamper proof" than stripe cards.

Box 1. From Credit Card to Smart Card – Transition or Revolution?
(cont'd)

The simplest smart cards are the so-called "stored-value" or "memory" cards. These can be used as telephone or cash cards – "charged" and "re-charged" to a fixed value and used-up as each transaction amount is deducted. At a more complex level, smart cards can be used for full credit card applications, and in a variety of "electronic purse" applications in which the smart card can be "charged" with varying amounts of cash, sometimes in several different currencies. Applications of this kind are particularly attractive for small transactions in that each exchange requires no costly verification procedure. It is possible, of course, to combine the credit and purse functions. To this end, Mastercard has recently acquired a majority interest in Mondex, a UK-based electronic purse provider.

Smart cards can also be used in a variety of roles as identification devices. In the GSM mobile telephone system, for example, all of the subscriber information necessary to authorise use of the system is contained on a smart card that can be transferred from terminal to terminal. There are also several existing and planned "advanced" smart-card applications. These include remote access cards containing tiny transmitters that can be read without requiring physical connections to a terminal, and "picture" cards that contain encoded photographs or even fingerprints. Smart cards of this type are already being used as industrial security devices, and their potential is being examined for applications like electronic ticketing, and even passport control.

Clearly, smart cards offer at least an interim solution to some of the problems of making consumer transactions more secure in an electronic environment. Wider smart-card access to commercial Internet services may be available soon as card readers for personal computers and television set-top boxes begin to proliferate. Nevertheless, smart cards are not always the preferred solution. The goal of some electronic ticketing schemes, for example, is to eliminate the need for customers to carry special cards, relying instead on centralised storage of booking information such that the customer can obtain the service by offering any form of identification.

Many believe that the future of the smart card as a payment system may depend on its adoption for a variety of other purposes – like personal identification and access to government services. Germany, now issues "smart" health insurance cards, and Spain has begun to issue "smart" combination Social Security/ID cards. Nevertheless, using smart cards in any role that could be considered an "identity card" will likely deter potential users in countries with a cultural aversion to carrying identity papers other than on a voluntary basis. Furthermore, the possibility of loss decreases the incentive for users to wish to integrate too many services on a single card.

3.   *The configuration of Electronic Commerce*

For Electronic Commerce to become operational, three basic configurations must be incorporated into a coherent functional structure. First, there is an *organisational configuration* involving the integration of business processes within and between the firms that produce and distribute goods and services that are traded in the electronic market-place. Second, there is a *network configuration* comprising the technological and administrative structures of electronic communications. In an Electronic Commerce context, the Internet has become an especially significant factor in this configuration. Third, there is a *media configuration* comprising the various technological devices that are used directly by buyers and sellers when transacting business electronically.

(a)   The organisational configuration: integrating business processes electronically

A business enterprise can be conceptualised as an interlinked system of information flows. Experience with the application of ICT to the automation of these flows has led many managers to advocate the strategic deployment of ICT to facilitate changes in the ways business processes are organised and made operational.[7]

Problems like reducing transaction costs cannot be addressed by technology alone. If the various "steps" in a transaction are to become compressed to various degrees, changes will be required in the organisation and management of enterprises. Different kinds of tasks will be defined and new skills required as more enterprises are "flattened" through the computerised integration of business processes.

As Electronic Commerce is primarily oriented to trade and exchange, the most difficult problem is to harmonize intra-organisational with *inter*-organisational business process integration. Figure 2 illustrates *four basic scenarios* for the electronic exchange of information within and between firms.[8]

Scenario One   (basic data exchange) – ICT links are established between specific business processes in transacting firms, but there is no electronic integration of business processes within the firms themselves.

Scenario Two (asymmetrical integration) – Selected business processes are integrated electronically within individual firms, but this integration is asymmetrical between transacting firms. Inter-firm data exchange remains configured as in Scenario One.

Scenario Three (symmetrical integration) – Similar business processes are integrated electronically between transacting firms, facilitating co-ordinated exchanges of data related to more than one business area.

Scenario Four (full integration) – All business processes are integrated electronically within and between transacting firms, permitting exchanges of all data related to all business areas.

There are, of course, many variations of these basic scenarios. Firms may use a common communication protocol, but different internal computer applications. Thus, the communication link might terminate at the application interfaces, requiring the reprocessing of data before they can be utilised by any firm.

In practice, moreover, there is not necessarily any momentum for sequential migration from Scenario One to Scenario Four. Many scenarios can operate concurrently, each supporting certain kinds of electronic transactions at some level. The degree of integration achieved can vary according to the type of enterprise, market or product involved, or according to the size and business scope of firms. Furthermore, even within firms, different business areas can be at different stages of process integration. Nevertheless, the full economies of an Electronic Commerce strategy can be achieved only if there is reasonable harmonization of business process integration between transacting firms.

For most firms wishing to exploit the full potential of Electronic Commerce, a practical goal would probably be to acquire the capability and flexibility to configure a Scenario Three relationship (including end-to-end applications interoperability) with any potential customer and/or supplier. This would allow a firm to make productive use of most available ICT systems to integrate core internal processes (*e.g.* EDI to link procurement with stock control) as well as to exchange data with suppliers and customers (*e.g.* electronic ordering in one firm co-ordinated with electronic invoicing in another). Firms can integrate internal processes with various resources that are shared with suppliers and product development partners – product management databases, computer aided design and manufacturing (CAD/CAM) capabilities, and so forth.

Figure 2. **Four Basic Scenarios for the Electronic Exchange of Information Between Firms**

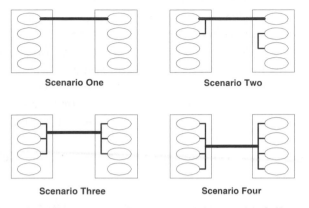

Scenario One   Scenario Two

Scenario Three   Scenario Four

Scenario Four describes an environment that would fully support both the customer and enterprise dimensions of Electronic Commerce. Currently, such a scenario remains exceptional. Several attempts are being made to construct highly integrated, transaction and product data systems for the collaborative development, manufacturing and logistics support of complex products like aircraft and defence systems. The best known of these initiatives is Continuous Acquisition and Life-cycle Support (CALS), originally developed by the US Department of Defense, but now being promoted widely as a general Electronic Commerce framework.[9] There are no concrete signs, however, that CALS or CALS-like approaches are meeting with widespread acceptance in industry as a whole.

The firms contacted by members of the Group indicated that business process integration is still an incremental process incorporating whatever tools are available. Firms remain wary of Scenario Four architectures that would tend to create lock-in to commercial relationships with specific partners. Currently, most of these firms would appear to occupy a position somewhere between Scenarios Two and Three, except in cases where ICT is being deployed to integrate specific design and production processes. As yet, no all purpose set of tools has emerged that will facilitate higher degrees of business integration, in ways that would be acceptable to a significant cross-section of industrial sectors.

(b)   The network configuration: providing a backbone for Electronic Commerce

Five years ago, it would have been a relatively straightforward task to describe the network facilities available for Electronic Commerce in terms of public and private voice and data telecommunication networks, and broadcast networks. These facilities remained structurally, and to some extent technologically separated. Even three years ago, as the idea of the "information superhighway" began to percolate in earnest throughout the business community, the corporate network topography was mostly viewed in terms of public and private dedicated data and voice circuits, and consumer-oriented Electronic Commerce was mostly viewed in terms of telemarketing and television shopping using toll-free telephone numbers.

Within the last couple of years, the growth of the Internet and the rapid development of its service base since the advent of the World Wide Web has changed dramatically the parameters of the debate about what an Electronic Commerce backbone network might look like. Furthermore, the corporate uptake of Internet capabilities has created a bifurcation in the Internet environment. There is now a public Internet sphere, accessible by anyone with an Internet connection to the public telecommunication network, and a private Internet sphere consisting of networks supported by the Internet Protocol, but operating wholly or partly within a closed corporate or inter-corporate communications structure. These private networks are referred to variously as "enterprise Internets", or "intranets" (sometimes as "extranets" where inter-corporate networking is involved) and they operate behind security firewalls. The amount of traffic in these private Internets now exceeds public Internet traffic.[10]

The Internet was not originally conceived in a commercial environment, however, and many of the particular administrative and technical elements required for trade and commerce have been slow to develop, or have developed in a very unco-ordinated fashion. Besides technical problems like bandwidth availability and network reliability, there have been serious problems in ensuring the security of commercial transactions on the Internet, and in coping with the real-time information exchange requirements of the electronic market-place. The major telecommunication providers can do much to improve this situation, as illustrated by the US case where the infrastructure has benefited recently from substantial investment in Asynchronous Transfer Mode (ATM) technology.

Nevertheless, the networking paradigm established by the Internet is clearly optimal for most Electronic Commerce applications, even if the present state of the facility is sub-optimal. The Internet is the first example of the kind of unitary communication vehicle that could eventually support commercial transactions at all levels of volume and complexity. The questions concern the kinds of commercially-oriented network configurations that might be possible within the Internet paradigm, and the kinds of safeguards and controls that might be necessary to support commercial activities.

(c) *The media configuration: gaining access to the electronic market-place*

Many communication media are potential doorways to the electronic market-place. In many countries, media like the telephone and television have had commercial orientations for a very long time. Until quite recently, however, the transactional capabilities of most of these were indirect. A consumer could be made aware of the existence, location and price of a product through television advertising, for example, but, in most cases, arrangements to obtain the product would have to be made by other means.

The three basic media domains currently available for Electronic Commerce are:

◊ telecommunication terminals (including fixed and mobile voice telephony, and fax);

◊ computer terminals (ranging from mainframes to PCs);

◊ broadcast terminals (comprising terrestrial, cable and satellite transmission).

The debate concerns the degree to which these media will remain exclusive of one another, converge into a multimedia environment, or even supplant one other. There has been much discussion, for example, of the merits of a television-based "network computer" concept, as an alternative to the Personal Computer.

Internet access is usually perceived in terms of the PC, but other forms of access must be taken seriously also. In 1995, about 60 per cent of US households had cable television connections, whereas just over 30 per cent had PCs (under a third of which were connected to modems).[11] Indeed, for certain types of Electronic Commerce services – like entertainment and home shopping

– the television environment is much more familiar to most consumers than the PC, and has the potential to offer much simpler interfaces to Internet-based Electronic Commerce applications. Furthermore, many cable and telephone networks will soon be able to provide virtually the same range of services. For example, in the United Kingdom, cable networks already provide much of the competition for basic telecommunication services and in Switzerland Internet access is provided via TV.

The overwhelming view of firms contacted by members of the Group was that changes in access media would have to be customer driven. Customers will gravitate to the medium that is easiest, quickest and most convenient to use, and prefer to stay with that medium until it is obvious to them that a different medium is superior. Many firms were of the view that the telephone (which has the largest penetration of any access medium in the OECD countries) would continue to be the preferred form of consumer access to many forms of Electronic Commerce services for some time to come. Further development of Electronic Commerce and other networking-based activities, however, requires that governments permit – and even encourage – the convergence of the different access technologies, ranging from telephone to television.

III. Issues and Opportunities in the Implementation of Electronic Commerce

The Group identified a number of issues that will be critical to the growth of Electronic Commerce, and that will likely require co-ordinated actions by industry and government. In the Group's view, addressing these issues is integral to the creation of new commercial opportunities in an electronic environment, as each issue is related in some way to increasing and sustaining levels of public trust and confidence in Electronic Commerce as a way of doing business. The Group identified four major issue areas – commercial, security, infrastructure, and socio-cultural – all of which are closely interconnected and reciprocal. In all four areas, many of the issues are legal, or have strong legal implications.

1. Commercial issues

Commerce depends on confidence. For the electronic market-place to flourish in both its customer and enterprise dimensions, buyers and sellers alike must have at least the level of confidence in the outcome of Electronic Commerce as they have in more traditional kinds of transactions. It must be possible for each participant in an electronic transaction to determine that both the transaction and the market environment in which it occurs are legitimate, in the sense that:

◊ the seller and buyer are who they claim to be;

◊ the seller has rights of sale over the item in question;

◊ the buyer has the resources to purchase the item;

◊ the transaction and payment mechanisms are available, legal and secure;

◊ the item sold corresponds to its description and is suitable for purpose;

◊ the purchased item (be it a product or service) can and will be delivered to the buyer.

Furthermore, transacting parties also expect to gain economically from a market environment that is open and competitive – not artificially distorted such that it favours some market actors over others.

All of these expectations give rise to some fundamental questions:

◊ Where does an electronic transaction actually take place in terms of contractual obligations, assignment of liabilities and tax responsibilities?

◊ Where are companies that trade electronically registered and regulated, and to which legal regimes are they subject?

◊ How are rights in tangible and intangible forms of property to be protected?

◊ What happens when a transaction goes wrong – who has responsibility and liability?

(a) *Consumer protection*

Although currently most Electronic Commerce exists at the enterprise level, much of the information gathered by the Group stressed the importance of the consumer interface in determining the future of Electronic Commerce. The

Internet is harmonizing the general environment in which electronic communications of all kinds take place. Thus, the electronic transaction environment is moving closer and closer to the individual. As more and more kinds of consumer transactions migrate to the electronic milieu, a number of issues become magnified that are fundamental to the creation of trust in Electronic Commerce as a way of doing business.

By definition, a product vendor using Electronic Commerce has no physical presence with respect to the consumer. In this respect, Electronic Commerce is different from the more established kinds of catalogue sales where the location and status of the trader can normally be determined, and, more importantly, a physical record normally exists of the product description and the transaction details. All of this can be missing from an electronic transaction, and, correspondingly, the possibilities for deception and fraud can increase. The non-territorial and intangible nature of Electronic Commerce calls into question the adequacy of existing law enforcement mechanisms that are still geared to tangible products and national legislation.

On the other hand, Electronic Commerce can also be used to document the transaction trail in great detail, and to process this information for product development and marketing purposes. This leads to questions about how to preserve the privacy of the consumer in an electronic environment (including the problem of aggressive direct solicitation). Vendors must also protect the confidentiality of information provided by the customer as part of a transaction. There are many legitimate purchases – medicines and professional services, for example – that consumers may prefer to keep confidential. Preserving consumer confidentiality involves the provision of mechanisms to prevent the use of transaction-generated information in ways that were not intended. It also involves ensuring that safeguards on the use of this information cannot be circumvented by the transportation of consumer databases between legal jurisdictions. At the moment, considerable discrepancies exist between the levels of data protection available in different countries.

A primary inhibitor to consumer use of Electronic Commerce facilities is the difficulty in locating the sources of products, and establishing liabilities, should these products be found not to be of the advertised quality, or not fit for the intended use. This situation is exacerbated where intangible products are involved. To overcome these problems, legal, administrative and technological mechanisms are needed to certify the identity of traders and the validity of guarantees and product descriptions, and to document electronically each stage in the transaction.

This could become an especially critical issue for new market entrants who have not already established a commercial reputation in the non-electronic market-place. One method, at least in the short to medium term, might be the use of endorsements. New product brands and vendors could enter the electronic market-place under the "umbrella" of a firm or brand name that has already established consumer trust in the market-place. Credit card firms and platform companies could also perform risk assessment, third party vetting, and rating of new companies. Endorsements could be certified electronically by means of an encrypted accreditation code. Current litigation practices, however, could inhibit development of the endorsement system, particularly in the United States.

Even when the purchasing part of the transaction is complete, consumers still have to be assured that they will receive the products they have purchased electronically in good order. At present, one of the weakest links in any consumer-oriented Electronic Commerce system involving tangible goods is the physical delivery infrastructure. Delivery can also be a problem for intangible products – entertainment and information services, for example – where the network backbone fails to provide access, or to deliver adequate bandwidth. In general, most types of on-demand delivery are expensive in most national markets, and these costs tend to increase over time. Business efficiencies realised at the supplier end through Electronic Commerce should result in more competitive prices to the consumer. These efficiencies can easily be wiped out by delivery costs, especially in countries where regulation keeps these charges artificially high.

(b)   Ensuring market diversity and competition

The members of the Group are committed to the principle that the electronic market-place should be open and competitive. Nevertheless, in preparing this Report, various actual and potential market barriers were noted that must be addressed if this principle is to be applied to the benefit of all buyers and sellers.

First, support for the principle of an open electronic market environment is not unambiguous. In migrating to this environment, incumbents want to preserve as much existing competitive advantage as they can. Moreover, incumbent companies may have an advantage in that they have already established consumer confidence in their trademarks and brand-names. As suggested in the previous section, this could be used to the advantage of new traders, but it is important that considerable emphasis is given to encouraging consumer confidence as soon as possible so that new electronic market entrants are not seriously disadvantaged.

Second, although examples can be found of successful Electronic Commerce operations that were launched with minimal investment, especially in the burgeoning Internet milieu, most firms find that considerable investment is now required to implement successful Electronic Commerce applications. Often the major part of this investment is not direct capital costs, but the associated costs of implementing and maintaining new systems and acquiring new technological and organisational competencies. For small and medium-sized enterprises (SMEs), these costs can take up a proportionally larger share of available investment capital than for large firms.

Third, although the theory holds that information technology should act to increase the flows of information available to buyers and sellers, the experience of firms contacted by the Group was that Electronic Commerce leads to an increased awareness of the value of information as a resource, and, consequently, to consolidations of partner networks, and reluctance to increase the variety of partners or to change them. Some correspondents noted that in an electronic milieu, price is becoming a less important factor in choosing suppliers than confidence based on prior experience with a supplier, and on existing levels of technological compatibility.

Finally, there is the possibility of retaliation by some retailers against companies that use Electronic Commerce to increase their volumes of direct sales to customers. The "by-passed" retailers (particularly if they are large chains) could take countervailing action to limit exposure of these products in the stores, leading suppliers to form consortia to break these retaliatory embargoes.

Box 2. Theory and Practice: Electronic Commerce and the Structure of Commercial Activities

It is clear from the discussion in this Report that Electronic Commerce has the potential profoundly to affect the structures and operations of markets and businesses. However, it is not a straightforward task to determine exactly *how* these structures might be affected.   The relationship between ICT implementation and general economic performance is only beginning to be understood.   Effects that can be observed at firm level are difficult to aggregate, and much of the available research is contradictory.[12] A major problem is that existing industrial output measures are still very much geared to production and distribution conditions defined primarily in terms of "material" products. As a result, research is only beginning to accumulate on the wider impacts of Electronic Commerce on the structure and productivity of the commercial system. An intriguing body of theory is emerging, but a much greater quantity and variety of intellectual input and empirical study is required. This Box presents some incipient ideas on the dynamics of commercial structures in an electronic environment.

1.   The market structure

One of the primary economic rationales for the application of ICT to commercial processes is that the quantity and quality of the information available to market participants can be increased.   In theory, greater symmetry in the information available to buyers and sellers should encourage economic structures in which product characteristics and prices are determined by market forces of supply and demand, rather than by management hierarchies.[13] In practice, however, there is a high degree of heterogeneity in the organisational and ICT profiles of different market actors, and the terms of entry into an electronically mediated commercial environment are seldom the same for each of them.   Past technology decisions determine different path dependencies with respect to the acquisition and diffusion of ICT in individual firms and industrial sectors. As different economic players may have very different starting positions when entering the electronic market-place, the challenge is to ensure that new barriers to market entry do not emerge.[14]

It is important to remember that the application of ICT to commercial processes does not, in itself, constitute Electronic Commerce. Electronic Commerce also involves the creation of new kinds of business and market structures. Each electronic market is a network, and setting up networks involves costs that must be recovered through efficiencies and/or through charges to buyers and sellers. Where there is an inchoate mass of buyers and sellers, the incentive will be to offer very open access terms in order to build up critical market mass in the network. Once critical mass exists, however, the incentive will be to focus the terms of access.   In well developed markets, many participants would pay an access premium in return for greater control over the transaction points in a commercial structure.[15]

Box 2. Theory and Practice: Electronic Commerce and the Structure of Commercial Activities *(cont'd)*

2. *The structure of the enterprise*

An electronic enterprise could exist solely as an entity in the network. It could be owned by a consortium based in several countries, and operated by a contractor utilising a variety of outsourced network facilities.   An Electronic Commerce environment will support many kinds of virtual organisations – short-term alliances of market actors assembled electronically to set up and complete a particular business transaction or industrial project.[16] Virtual organisations can be structured flexibly such that market players can enter and exit the structure easily as their products or services are required.   At some point, however, especially in complex transactions, management structures will emerge that operate as virtual hierarchies. In the absence of technological and administrative safeguards, these virtual hierarchies can become entrenched, thus inhibiting new market entrants.

3. *The price structure*

It has always been characteristic of the market system that different local conditions may support different prices for otherwise identical goods, and that sellers are free to compete on price provided that they do not subsidise price discounts on terms that are unfair to other participants in the market.   Hypothetically, a globalised electronic market-place could allow a potential buyer to locate the lowest available price for a given product anywhere in the world, and to locate it quickly. Provided that ordering, payment and delivery structures also existed, the customer could then acquire the product at the lowest world price, thus circumventing the conditions in his or her own local market, save, perhaps, for taxes and delivery costs.   The degree to which widespread Electronic Commerce could eventually harmonize the global price structure, is still a matter for debate. However, the rapidity with which buyers could perform thorough reconnaissance of available prices could be enough in itself to have a significant harmonizing effect on local price structures, with subsequent effects on cost structures.

4. *Intermediation*

It can be argued that as one of the aims of Electronic Commerce is to truncate the steps in a transaction, many forms of intermediation will become unnecessary. This is an oversimplification.   Certainly, there could be an increase in direct sales in an electronic environment, thus eliminating many traditional retailing and wholesaling operations, but most of the steps in a transaction will still require institutional and distribution support of some kind. However, the kinds of intermediation required to support commerce in intangible products and services will certainly be of a different kind than those traditionally associated with tangible products. Indeed, many forms of Electronic Commerce may not be sustainable unless new forms of intermediation develop to support the customer/supplier relationship.[17] In some circumstances, ntermediation can reduce transaction costs by adding value to product information and co-ordinating transaction support structures such as contract negotiation, credit, insurance, funds transfer and logistics. Indeed, one of the growth business areas in an electronic market-place could well be in the field of intermediation – setting up businesses that co-ordinate all of the support mechanisms necessary to preserve buyer and seller confidence in the market.

5.   *Substitution*

As firms become involved extensively in Electronic Commerce, and new business forms begin to evolve, it becomes increasingly difficult to determine which rules apply to which enterprise. There are now many examples of business substitution, where firms have found that their intangible products have become as profitable or more profitable than tangible products. Thus, retailers become major sellers of insurance and credit, transportation firms generate substantial revenues from reservation services, and engineering firms build up new businesses around logistics systems. There are also examples of substitution within the intangible environment, as when telephone companies become cable television companies. The role of technology in enabling business substitution to occur with greater frequency and rapidity, is causing many to question the established theory that firms exist primarily to manage costs, and to propose that firms exist to organise learning processes and to manage change.[18] Business substitution is likely one of the principal ways in which Electronic Commerce can contribute to the creation of jobs.

(c)   Financial and payment systems

Financial services exist to protect, invest and manage money. The range of financial products is huge – from personal banking to the management of complex international investment portfolios. Payment systems transfer money from buyers to sellers. The simplest system is the physical exchange of cash, but the volumes and complexities of transactions, even at the personal level, have spawned a huge variety of methods to transfer funds for commercial purposes – cheques, direct debits, credit cards and electronic funds transfer to name only a few.

Most financial and payment system issues intersect important areas of government policy and regulation – particularly regarding currency flows and customer risk. Electronic Commerce raises many new issues in this respect in that not only does it require new approaches to financial activities that are already regulated and for which policies exist, but it sets up a number of situations for which there is currently no control regime at all unless voluntary. In some cases, industry may prefer to adopt internal controls, but in others, particularly where it is necessary to instil confidence amongst a wide spectrum of interests, external regulation may be required. Requirements for external regulation will become more clear as competitive experience is gained in the electronic market-place.

In an Electronic Commerce environment, financial services and products (banking, insurance, investments, etc.) can be obtained from virtually anywhere, and it can be difficult for the user of these services to ensure that the suppliers are legitimate, or to assess the level of risk that may be involved. In the electronic market-place, a customer could believe he or she was purchasing a product from a firm registered in his or her own country (thereby subject to its laws and regulations) only to find that the product emanated from a foreign subsidiary, sharing the same corporate identity, but subject to a different regime of controls and not necessarily guaranteed by the parent. Financial regulations vary considerably from country to country, but rights and obligations are generally not transferable from one country to another. This situation not only creates risk for the customer, it also may limit opportunities for financial services firms to develop international markets using Electronic Commerce.

Although examples are already beginning to appear of the use of electronic currencies – so-called "cybercash" or "e-cash" – for the settlement of accounts, it may well be that concerted action by public and private sector financial institutions will be necessary for the security of electronic settlement systems to be assured so that buyers and sellers will have confidence in them. At one level, the payment system is a network security problem in that transacting parties must be confident that electronic transfers of funds will not be diverted and that the amount received will be the amount agreed – and cryptography may be employed to enhance the security of payments. At deeper levels, however, payment systems are subject to a plethora of economic and legal pressures.

A basic issue, particularly for consumer transactions, is the problem of being able to match monetary amounts with the most cost-effective payment infrastructure. All payment systems involve costs that need to be recovered in some way if the system is to be sustainable. In the credit card industry, there has always been cross-subsidy between credit profits and transaction costs, thus enabling the same card to be used for large and small transactions, even though the costs are proportionally greater for the smaller amounts than for the larger ones. As Electronic Commerce payment requirements become more diverse and sophisticated, new methods will be necessary to meet the costs of payment systems. Electronic purse services are already available that lower the administration costs of processing small electronic payments.

Although payment systems can preserve a considerable degree of confidentiality, no current system offers complete anonymity. There are both legal and commercial requirements for the auditability of payment systems – *i.e.* to ensure that the source, route and destination of each payment can be identified. Concern is already high that Electronic Commerce facilities could offer increased opportunities to criminals, both to transfer illegally obtained funds from place to place, and to engage in money laundering.[19] These concerns are exacerbated in that some new network and card-based e-cash technologies might permit truly anonymous transactions. Vendors are concerned that security problems with anonymous payment systems may inhibit their development.

Many currently believe that anonymous smart-card-based e-cash will only be used for small transactions. Furthermore, with smart-card technology, some governments may fix limits on the amounts permitted to be held on cash cards and on the amounts permitted to cross borders. One of the practical outcomes announced in connection with the recent merger of Mastercard and Mondex, an electronic purse company, is that combining the cash and credit card systems may expand the audit trails for smaller transactions according to the limits set by national regulators. Mondex have at all stages voluntarily sought advice from the Bank of England.[20]

Most importantly, the status of many of these new payment concepts with respect to the existing financial system is uncertain. The broader economic and legal implications of financial and payment systems that might operate (even partially) outside the banking system, are not entirely clear.[21] Potentially, they have considerable significance for monetary and fiscal policies, and the determination of financial liabilities.

(d)   Taxation

Unlike most previous market innovations, the transnational and intangible nature of Electronic Commerce has especially direct implications for the ability of governments to raise revenues through established mechanisms like sales and corporate taxes, value added taxes and tariffs. There is currently much discussion about the possibilities of government revenue loss owing to the increased use of electronic media for commercial purposes. Moreover, international price harmonization effects as a result of Electronic Commerce, should they occur, may affect the national tax base. The international and

51

intangible characteristics of Electronic Commerce suggest to many that it may open up avenues that legally circumvent national tax structures altogether, as well as facilitating outright tax evasion and fraud.

The main concern of the Group is not that electronic transactions will be subject to tax, but that the tax regime employed is workable and non-discriminatory. A further concern is the possibility that some firms could gain unfair advantages by operating from tax havens. It is important to examine the taxation question carefully, as fiscal policies can have major effects on market environments, particularly new ones like Electronic Commerce. Some governments have already opened up a fiscal dialogue with industry concerning the implications of Electronic Commerce for taxation, but most are only beginning to consider the problem.

There are two basic sales taxation scenarios in Electronic Commerce: *i)* collecting tax related to tangible goods ordered by electronic means, and *ii)* collecting tax on intangible exchanges. On the other hand, there is an enormous world-wide complex of types of taxes, and collection regimes. Relationships between national tax regimes are almost all bilateral and reciprocal agreements that are prone to avoidance loopholes. Moreover, governments themselves are not unambiguously in favour of open electronic markets, in that in many areas (airline ticketing, for example) governments virtually compete for "tax sales". As cross-border Electronic Commerce transactions are escalating all the time, an internationally applied system is required but the complexities and ambiguities of the tax regime are likely to delay negotiations.

Producers and distributors of all kinds have fulfilled a tax collection role for many years – virtually all production- and consumption-related taxes are collected by business and industry on behalf of government. In an Electronic Commerce environment, this role may increase, and it may be developed into a significant business area in its own right.

The problem in a intangible environment is "who gets taxed where?" or "does anyone get taxed?". One revealing example is evident in countries where there are different provinces or states with different sales taxes. Telephone and mail order firms resident in one state are typically not required to collect the taxes imposed in another. Although purchasers may have the legal responsibility to pay these taxes, few do, and the transactions are normally impossible to police. A similar situation exists for cyber-firms except that the nature of the network on which the transaction takes place allows re-interpretation of who is resident where. In the United States, for example, many states are now arguing that any

Internet service provider in any state is the legal agent of any firm that uses the Internet to sell goods, irrespective of the place of registration for that firm. If this argument is won, every cyber-firm will be considered to be liable to collect local taxes in every state in which it does business, provided it knows where the purchaser is.

Many believe that situations such as the above will create an impossible commercial environment and that serious traders will simply move their operations off-shore. For tangible goods, however, such a move might actually make it easier for governments to recover the tax at the point of entry for the goods in question. Intangible goods provide a greater problem, but even here, various technologies are under development (IBM's "cryptolope" concept, for example) that possibly could be adapted for use in identifying and determining the taxable value and origin of intangible merchandise.

One high-profile proposal is to tax not the product or service, but rather to tax the transmission of data involved in the transaction. In theory, the "bit tax" could eliminate most of the tax advantages of off-shore operations. The idea has already attracted significant attention in the European Union. However, there are many problems with the bit tax proposal. Volumes of traffic cannot be accurately measured (nor can they always be attributed), rendering the bit tax easy to circumvent technologically. Data might be measured for tax purposes at its source or destination, but not during flow. There is a major problem in ascribing value to data, and, correspondingly, in determining what should be taxable and what should not. There is also the problem of asymmetry, in that the bit tax would apply to Electronic Commerce transactions, when other kinds of transactions (mail-order sales, for example) could continue to flourish outside the tax net. Furthermore, a bit tax could bring many forms of data exchange related to the non-transactional aspects of Electronic Commerce or pure e-mail unjustifiably into the tax net. A vast volume of corporate data exchange is unrelated to any function that is taxed under current regimes.

(e)   Intellectual Property Rights (IPR)

Intellectual property issues are becoming more and more important to an increasing range of business activities. In an electronic environment, commercial firms have a heightened awareness of the need to be able to protect trademarks and commercial information held in databases. They are also becoming more aware of the links between IPR and the innovation process, and concerned that any changes in the IPR system do not present unreasonable obstacles to the development of Electronic Commerce.

The current international regimes for the protection of IPRs are geared to "ideas", and, specifically, to the expression of ideas in physical media – print, sound recordings, video and motion pictures, etc. The challenge for governments is to redefine these regimes such that they are better able to cope with electronic information services. Currently, the IPR regime is separated structurally between copyright for literary properties, and patents for technological specifications and processes. Moreover, on the copyright side, IPR enforcement responsibilities are divided among different institutions, each with an orientation towards specific reproduction media. This institutional structure makes less and less sense as media converge.

The spread of electronic networking has called the adequacy of IPR definition and protection arrangements into question. A debate has emerged, for example, as to whether computer programs, currently protected under copyright provisions, can contain algorithms that might also be entitled to patent protection. New challenges exist also for the enforcement function of the IPR system, as electronically distributed information is highly prone to casual and undetectable copying and re-distribution. IPR policies will have to be synchronised with encryption policies.

2.   Security issues

The term "security" encompasses a very wide range of issues, but the main security concerns for Electronic Commerce are the protection of availability, confidentiality and integrity of information systems and the data that is stored and transmitted. First, the security of the networks themselves must be ensured. This involves quality of service provisions to ensure that network facilities for Electronic Commerce are robust and available as needed, and that unauthorised or malicious access to networks is minimised. Second, the security of commercial messages and network-based transactions must be ensured. This means ensuring that data and information is only disclosed to authorised persons, entities and process, and that it is accurate and complete and has not been modified or altered in an unauthorised manner.

Probably the most central goal of any security scheme is to protect the integrity of transaction related information. Any kind of message can be intercepted, but intercepted electronic messages can be altered in ways that could be imperceptible to the intended receiver. Without safeguards, the potential for alteration can call into question the "authenticity" of electronic messages – *i.e.* "Is the content as read by the intended receiver the same as that provided by the original sender?" It is also important that each transacting party can confirm the identity and status of the other. In an electronic environment, logos, brand-names and trademarks are easy to replicate, and it can be easy for buyers and sellers to misrepresent their financial and legal status, or even their physical locations.

Box 3. What is "Cryptography" and Why is it an Issue?[22]

Cryptography for confidentiality and integrity of data

Historically, cryptography has been used to encode information to conceal secret messages from unauthorised parties and, as such, it has traditionally been important for military and national security use. Cryptography uses an algorithm to transform data in order to render it unintelligible to anyone who does not have the cryptographic "key" necessary for decryption of the data. Today, the availability of increased calculation power makes it possible to use complex mathematical algorithms for encryption of data. In the mid-1970s new uses for cryptography were developed and it became an information security tool with broader applications – these developments moved cryptography into the private sector domain. Some of these new uses for cryptography play an important role in developing information infrastructures with the potential to accommodate electronic commerce and become strategic tools for confidential transmission and safeguarding the integrity of data in an open network environment in which parties do not know one another in advance. In addition, since open networks such as the Internet present significant challenges for making enforceable electronic contracts and security payments, cryptography may contribute to the solution of both of these problems by providing mechanisms for establishing the validity of a claimed identity of a user, device or another entity in an information system ("authentication") and for preventing an individual or entity from denying having performed a particular action related to data ("non-repudiation").

The cryptography debate

A critical issue presented by cryptography – perhaps the most widely debated aspect of cryptography and the one most likely to lead to disparate national regulation – is the perceived conflict between the use of cryptography for confidentiality and the concern of governments that this will limit their ability to protect public safety and national security.

At the present time, security issues have immediate economic consequences for users of Electronic Commerce applications in that the level of security that can be provided is often dependent upon the kind of network employed. This limits choice and the opportunity to lower costs. Open networks like the Internet generally provide much less security than "dedicated" network links. This limits Internet use in commercial situations even though it may offer distinct economic advantages to buyers and sellers in terms of access charges and flexibility of use. In the air transport industry, the concerns about interception and alteration inhibit airlines from expanding their use of the Internet to access manufacturer documentation, thus tying them into an expensive leased-line environment.

The OECD has been active for some time in the area of security of information systems. The 1992 OECD Guidelines for the Security of Information Systems[23] identified the need for technological means to assure security of information systems. During 1996 the OECD has been engaged in drafting Guidelines for Cryptography Policy[24] to identify the issues which should be taken into consideration in the formulation of cryptography policies at the national and international level. These guidelines have been developed in recognition of the increasing dependency of OECD countries on electronic information systems, and the increasingly important social, political and economic consequences of vulnerability in these systems.

Industry is taking a leading role in addressing these concerns but a general security framework for Electronic Commerce has still not been achieved. The "Secure Electronic Transactions" (SET) initiative that is being worked out between several of the major international payment systems and suppliers such as Microsoft and IBM attracts much attention, but many questions remain about the economics of SET, and about the technological and administrative dimensions of making SET interoperable between industrial sectors. Moreover, it is likely that alternatives and complements to SET will emerge.

(a)   How secure is "secure"?

Electronic commerce offers great opportunities for the business community and consumers, however it also brings with it some significant risks. The explosive world-wide growth of open networks has raised a legitimate concern with respect to the adequacy of security measures for information and communications systems and the data which is transmitted and stored on those systems. The developing information infrastructure is a fertile environment for all kinds of computer-related crime, including fraud and privacy infringement, thus prompting demands for effective data security measures. Both technical and legal solutions are required to replace in the electronic environment the physical security of the paper-based world. It is important that solutions are trustworthy and that users and consumers have confidence in them.

Any security system can be broken, and the worst intruders are often insiders. Probably the least effective way to instil public confidence in the security of networked transactions is to make blanket assertions that networks are completely secure. Rather, confidence building is dependent upon maintaining the public perception that the levels of security provided for each type of data exchange are reasonable and adequate, that breaches can be detected quickly, that corrective action can be taken, and that the lines of responsibility between transacting and intermediary parties are clearly defined.

The expense involved in providing security must be weighed against the security expectations of transacting parties. No bank is immune from robbery, for example, but this does not dissuade depositors as long as they perceive the likelihood of sustaining severe personal losses due to robbery to be remote. Credit card companies generally work out the economics of increased security against an evaluation of what they can afford to absorb in fraud losses each year. For customers, the convenience of the credit card system may overshadow other considerations as long as the costs do not exceed a sustainable level, that defensive mechanisms exist to minimise the security problem, and that the liabilities of individual customers can be limited.

Indeed, customer attitudes to security in general are varied and sometimes ambiguous. Individuals make purchases over the telephone using credit cards, with little knowledge about the security of these transactions, and some seem already prepared to use credit cards on the Internet even though there was virtually no security at all for Internet transactions until very recently. A firm that expresses concerns about the security of "on-line" transactions may completely overlook the negative security implications of transaction media like the telephone and fax machine, simply because these media are more familiar.

Much of the discussion about security revolves around the issue of *"cryptography"*, and especially the different attitudes of national governments as to the terms under which cryptography should be provided. Cryptography is an important component of secure information and communications systems and a variety of applications have been developed that incorporate cryptographic technologies to provide data security. Cryptography is an effective tool for ensuring both the confidentiality and the integrity of data, and each of these uses offers certain benefits. However, the widespread use of cryptography raises other important issues, and cryptography policy must balance a number of varied interests. In addition to its role in the operation of electronic commerce, cryptography has implications for the protection of privacy, intellectual property, business and financial information, as well as public safety and national security. Many believe that until government policies concerning cryptography are harmonized internationally, the growth prospects for Electronic Commerce will be damaged.

Cryptography is certainly a necessary part of any security system, but adequate security is not provided by the use of cryptography alone. The best cryptography in the world will not protect a network that is otherwise vulnerable because of design faults or careless procedures that leave critical interfaces exposed to intruders (this includes non-electronic interfaces as well as electronic ones). Ultimately, security is as much an organisational matter as it is a technological problem. Moreover, the relative priority and significance of security measures vary according to the information or the information system.

(b)   The institutional aspects of security

The important task for developers of EC applications is to foster an environment in which public confidence in security arrangements for electronic transactions will grow. This is partly a matter of employing the best available security devices in networks that are thoroughly designed with security in mind. It is also a matter of providing an institutional framework that can support various security functions.

Institutional evolution will be required in three main areas:

> *(i) Authentication/Non-repudiation/Data integrity.* There is a tremendous potential for fraud in the electronic world. Transactions take place at a distance without the benefit of physical clues that permit identification, making impersonation easy. The ability to make perfect copies and undetectable alterations of digitised data complicates the matter. Traditionally hand-written signatures serve to determine the authenticity of an original document. In the electronic world, the concept of an "original" document is problematic, but a "digital signature" – using cryptography – can verify data integrity, and provide authentication and non-repudiation functions to certify the sender of a message. If a document itself has been altered in any way after it has been signed, the digital signature will so demonstrate. Similarly, once a person signs a document with a cryptographic

key, the digital signature provides proof that the document was signed by the purported author, and the sender cannot deny having sent the document or claim that the information has been altered during transmission. The same technology can be applied to ensuring the authenticity and integrity of documents archived electronically. New regulations are needed concerning the registration and use of digital signatures and the liability of issuing authorities, and proposals have already been made by the American Bar Association.

(ii)Certification. The identity and many of the characteristics of transacting parties can be validated using certification procedures – usually by a third party that acts as a "certification authority" to provide information about the transacting parties. Certification is necessary to ensure that transacting parties are who they say they are, but also that they will be able to provide the level of security necessary to complete the transaction safely. On the identity side, certification encompasses the problem of "watermarking" – ensuring that electronic "representations" of identity, like logos and trademarks, are in fact genuine. At present, these devices can be forged with great ease in an electronic environment. On the security side, certification is necessary to ensure that any form of security protection that is claimed by a transacting party will actually be provided by that party – as in "firewall" certification, etc. At this level, certification becomes an issue of trading standards and business ethics.

However, the certificate authority itself must be reliable, so the certifier may need to be certified. This issue could be addressed by both a hierarchy of certificate authorities and a system of cross-certified certificate authorities. Governments must assume responsibility for providing the legal framework for the registration of companies and this must be linked at some point to certification procedures. It is open to question, however, whether governments should become involved directly in actual certification procedures. This is a function that could be undertaken effectively by private sector organisations. Indeed, in the United States, the Better Business Bureau and CommerceNet have plans to become involved in the certification of companies that trade electronically. The extent to which, at the international level, independent international management frameworks for certification may be required in addition to national arrangements is also open to question.

(iii)*Data protection.* The use of networks for commercial transactions increasingly generates vast quantities of data that can be easily and cheaply stored, analysed and reused, and neither open networks, nor many types of private networks, were designed with communications and storage confidentiality in mind. For Electronic Commerce to thrive in a commercial environment governed by the principles of open markets and free trade, participants in a market must be able to exchange commercial data freely across national boundaries, confident that there will be no unauthorised access to this information. In 1980, the OECD published guidelines which addressed the protection of privacy and transborder flows of personal data[25]; while these guidelines have stood the test of time and are still applicable today, the implications for this issue have expanded in proportion to the explosive growth in digital computer processing and network technologies. Governments are challenged to balance the growing commercial requirement to exchange data of all kinds securely across national borders, and the needs of governments to control and regulate data flows in relation to concerns such as privacy protection or security. Both the public and private sector need to address this issue by implementing appropriate technical and organisation measures to protect personal data against accidental loss, alteration, abuse and unauthorised movement between countries, disclosure or access, in particular where data is transmitted over a network.

3.   *Infrastructure issues*

The Group collected a wide range of observations on the infrastructure problems associated with the development of Electronic Commerce. It is clear that many wide variations persist in the technical capabilities and administrative conditions of national telecommunication systems, and that the current electronic networking environment is full of anomalies. It was noted, for example, that essential communications for airline safety and maintenance (service bulletins and air worthiness directives) are sent out on Telex as this is still the only infrastructure with any real claim to being available anywhere in the world. It was noted also that much of the data exchange in the insurance industry is still accomplished by the physical transport of tapes, not because data communication facilities do not exist, but because physical transport is often cheaper and quicker than telecommunications.

Given the front-runner status of the Internet as the first networking environment capable of achieving a widespread presence in virtually all areas of Electronic Commerce, an immediate goal is the development of a managed Internet backbone – a secure, widely accessible, fully interconnected high speed international network that will guarantee the availability of bandwidth sufficient for the requirements of Electronic Commerce. A recent survey suggested that currently less than five per cent of US corporate network managers are using Internet as the backbone of their wide area networks, and nearly three-quarters of managers surveyed reported no plans to migrate to Internet in the near future.[26] This response is partly due to the fact that firms have already made significant technology investments, and must maximise their returns on these investments. Nevertheless, it is also due to the many residual technological and administrative constraints that still inhibit the growth of network services markets.

(a)   Network capacity

Even in the most advanced countries, growth in available bandwidth is generally much too slow to promote Electronic Commerce as a universal market access medium. The bandwidth problem is even worse in a "mobile data" environment, potentially a high growth area for Electronic Commerce. Estimates provided by Deutsche Telekom indicate that data communication makes up less than 5 per cent of digital cellular traffic. Growth is inhibited by the scarcity of available radio frequencies, and by lack of international harmonization in the current technical and administrative regimes. The bandwidth problem in both fixed and mobile networks is exacerbated by tariff structures that are not cost- or usage-based. It is important to establish more realistic pricing regimes, especially considering that, in the long term, rapid growth in traffic volumes will mean that telecommunication costs for Electronic Commerce are likely never actually to decline in total terms. Ultimately, it is expected that the increase in data flows will continue to outrun the decline in data transfer costs.

(b)   Network access

Most Internet applications run on telephone lines in the public network, but the persistence of restrictive national regulatory structures remains a major inhibitor to the provision of Internet services in many markets. Furthermore, in most countries, public telecommunication operators are still not oriented to the networking needs of Electronic Commerce. Operators prefer to offer value-added services rather than backbone management as such. This has encouraged the exploration of alternative media for Internet access – particularly satellite and cable television systems. In the United States, there is more diversity in approaches. While the main telecommunication companies offer new ATM-based infrastructures, the @Home initiative plans to develop a nation-wide managed Internet backbone by utilising the facilities of many local cable television companies. This system is intended to provide a facility for secure commercial transactions on the Internet. With the growth of cable systems, particularly in Europe, the concept could eventually extend beyond the United States. In most markets, in any case, use of the cable networks for Electronic Commerce will require substantial investments in order to re-engineer these facilities to provide two-way capabilities.

A recent OECD study has shown that there is a relationship between the degree of openness in the telecommunication markets in OECD countries and the penetration and pricing of Internet access. In 1995, leased line Internet access in countries with no infrastructure competition was 44 per cent higher than in countries allowing infrastructure competition. Likewise, dial-up access charges were three times as expensive in markets with no competition.[27]

(c)   *Network development*

The Internet was designed for resilience, but not for security, ease of use, or even reliability. This must change, but change may not come easily. In general, Internet service providers (ISP) do not invest at levels that are necessary to support Electronic Commerce. Employing "quick fixes" in pursuit of immediate returns will not result in an increase in the overall quality or reliability of the Internet. Internet-based solutions to business networking problems are being developed by a variety of software houses, systems integrators, and even content providers. Applications and software developers are continually demonstrating that the performance envelope of the existing Internet environment can be expanded considerably. In many cases, however, this merely exacerbates the backbone management problem. It is likely that the impetus for managed network development internationally will emerge not from the public Internet, but from the proliferation of private Internets. Some ISPs may move into the intranet and extranet environments.

(d)   *Standards*

Electronic Commerce intersects the domains of telecommunications, broadcasting and computing. Each domain has different institutional structures for the development of technical standards for the interconnection and interpretability of network technologies. In many cases, these structures are reinforced by separate regulatory regimes. Furthermore, each of these domains has different attitudes towards standardization – the computer sector being far more amenable to a mixture of proprietary and non-proprietary standards than the telecommunication and broadcasting sectors. Existing standards institutions are still focused on standards requirements for "electronic data processing" (EDP) and EDI, and have yet to engage fully with the standardization requirements of Electronic Commerce as defined and described in this Report.

Although some progress is being made on the harmonization of standards for core services like EDI, these standards are still inadequate even after many years of development. Many other Electronic Commerce service environments are similarly bedevilled by a plethora of partially compatible or incompatible standards.[28] Many now expect that EDI, as a paradigm, may give way to a variety of Internet-based approaches to data transfer, thus heralding the end of standards frameworks like EDIFACT and X.12. Eventually, however, a more extended range of standards may be required for Electronic Commerce – standardized electronic contract formats, for example, or standardized protocols for the exchange of technical and product specifications.

Although many of the firms contributing to this study identified the need for more and better standards for Electronic Commerce, it is clear that some types of business are more amenable than others to the standardization of different Electronic Commerce elements. In manufacturing industries, for example, internationally standardized formats for commodity descriptions would expedite commercial transactions considerably. In the insurance industry, on the other hand, customers choose products more on evaluations of insurer quality than on "trade descriptions" of products, or even price. For products that are not commodities, national or international standards may be so difficult to negotiate that emerging *de facto* standards will have to be accepted.

4.   *Social and cultural issues*

Commercial relationships are shaped to a considerable extent by social conditions and cultural attitudes. The Group noted that diffusion of the benefits and opportunities of Electronic Commerce could be limited by factors such as language, social attitudes, and conditions of access to the ICT infrastructure. It is already a fact, for example, that most of the commercial and non-commercial services on the Internet are oriented to the English language, and that Internet access is heavily concentrated in a handful of highly developed economies.

Also noted were concerns about the effects of Electronic Commerce on social behaviour, and in particular, the problem of network content that raises moral, political and social objections in different cultural settings.

The Group was highly sympathetic to these concerns, not least because responsiveness to social and cultural conditions is recognised as an important factor in building commercial relationships of all kinds. Nevertheless, it is quickly becoming impossible for firms, countries and individuals to avoid the impacts of Electronic Commerce, irrespective of the degree to which they participate in it directly. The issue of information "haves" and "have nots" is a crucial one for Electronic Commerce, and it applies to individuals as well as countries and regions, especially in the newly industrialising and developing world.

The characteristics and implications of Electronic Commerce will inevitably produce social and cultural pressures. At this point, however, there is great uncertainty about the form these pressures will take and how serious they will be in terms of maintaining social stability. There is urgent need on an international basis to monitor the social and cultural changes that are occurring in response to the proliferation of electronic services of all kinds, including Electronic Commerce.

IV.   The Role of Government in Electronic Commerce

1.   *How are government and industry agendas linked for electronic commerce?*

Governments have a direct stake in Electronic Commerce by virtue of the fact that in virtually every country, the public sector is the largest single procurer of goods and services. Increasingly, moreover, the general trend in most countries is for government to seek private-sector sources for as many products and services as possible. Even where government requirements are highly specialised (defence, for example), the trend is to insist on off-the-shelf and dual-use products wherever possible.

As governments seek to increase their own implementations of Electronic Commerce solutions, they become subject to the same kinds of pressures for organisational and managerial change as do private firms. In government, the concept of Electronic Administration is evolving in a somewhat symbiotic relationship with the development of Electronic Commerce. Together, these forces are bringing many of the interests of government and industry closer together, both with respect to the benefits and the problems of Electronic Commerce.

In many respects, interaction between the public and private sectors is an important driver of Electronic Administration principles in government. The private sector is making increasing demands for the simplification of interactions with government agencies, and the harmonization of transaction procedures. On the other hand, the procurement power of governments places them in especially strong positions to influence the development of new commercial technologies and practices. In many OECD countries, public procurement agencies have been amongst the most prominent advocates of "open" systems for electronic networking, and have been major backers of EDI, encouraging its use in the private sector. In the less advanced countries, these same Electronic Administration drivers intensify pressures to adjust to international best practice. It is often at those points that require continuous interactions between the public and private sectors that these forces begin to reciprocate. Treasury departments, customs and excise, and tax agencies, for example, are often the first to develop sophisticated data communication links with the private sector.

2.   What can governments do to promote Electronic Commerce?

Governments can play two positive roles in the development of Electronic Commerce:

Direct promotion through applications of Electronic Commerce principles in government administration and procurement, and in the provision of public services.

Facilitation of the development of Electronic Commerce through the provision of a legal, regulatory and infrastructural environment that encourages the development of Electronic Commerce.

The choice of government roles, or, more usually, the blend of roles, can depend on many factors. In countries where the private sector has already taken a lead in Electronic Commerce, government can support these initiatives by providing a supportive legal and regulatory environment, and by ensuring that government administration practices are sensitive to the characteristics of the electronic market-place. Some examples of governmental and intergovernmental initiatives by some of the highly developed economies are outlined in Annex A.

In the case of newly industrialising and developing countries, governments should be encouraged to take a creative role in promoting Electronic Commerce. In these contexts, public interventions of various kinds can act as important catalysts for the diffusion of Electronic Commerce applications in the private sector.

Singapore provides a good example of the kind of productive symbiosis that can exist between the public and private sectors in the development of Electronic Commerce. In this case, a national policy initiative has been undertaken, aimed at giving Singapore a "head start" on its trading partners in the provision of infrastructure (the "wired intelligent island") and the restructuring of business processes. The Singapore government is taking direct action to encourage Electronic Commerce by initiating a government-wide electronic procurement system. Governments can act also to encourage the application of Electronic Commerce to key national economic institutions. In India, for example, recent government legislation to encourage the creation of new stock exchanges has led to the establishment of the fully electronic National Stock Exchange.

In whatever roles governments choose to take, however, it is essential that these roles be clearly visible and understood both within government and in private business. The function of "chief information officer" (CIO) has much the same role in government as in industry. In the same way as a corporate CIO provides an enterprise-wide ICT perspective to individual business units, government CIOs should provide an overall perspective on ICT deployment in the public sector. This CIO function can provide a valuable "pivot" for the development of productive government-industry relationships in Electronic Commerce.

3.   *Defining the policy and regulatory agenda for Electronic Commerce*

Over time, the market system has developed a sophisticated structure of private and public sector institutions to develop and enforce rules governing the conduct of transactions. The objective in sustaining this structure is to maintain trust in the commercial system. Many of the established principles of market governance apply also to the electronic market-place, although new ways must be found to articulate and make them function in an electronic milieu. In other cases, however, the electronic environment challenges the efficacy of existing structures, or questions their necessity altogether.

In the modern era, governments have exercised controls over the commercial environment for two principal reasons. Firstly, governments have sought to

66

prevent abuses of the market system through such measures as competition policy and the regulation of financial institutions. Secondly, governments have sought to promote commercial environments aimed at yielding particular social and economic outcomes, using such measures as foreign investment and exchange policies, consumer protection legislation, or skills and training programmes. In many cases, initiatives to impose controls have come from business and industry as well as from government itself, and the original objectives of most of these controls was to institutionalise conditions of trust between buyers and sellers.

However, most of the legal and regulatory mechanisms currently being applied by governments to commercial activity were conceived in an era before the advent of advanced electronic communication systems. The majority of these mechanisms are national in orientation. Even where international instruments and institutions exist, their main function is to support the sovereign rights of national governments. Moreover, frameworks of commercial policy, law and regulation are still oriented overwhelmingly to trade in tangible goods.

As documented in this Report, Electronic Commerce has the propensity to ignore sector and national boundaries, and it tends to accentuate the intangible aspects of commerce over the tangible aspects. This presents a policy challenge for governors and governed alike. Both must face a rapidly escalating economic phenomenon with which they have limited experience, and over which they have uncertain powers of control. They must be prepared to act in concert, where appropriate, lest poorly co-ordinated actions stifle the development of Electronic Commerce before its full potential becomes evident.

The entire basis of commercial policy making is now coming under close scrutiny. Electronic Commerce presents many fundamental challenges to the policy framework, especially where the enforcement of legal and regulatory provisions is concerned. Governance of the electronic market-place is certainly beyond the scope of action for individual governments, requiring instead an increased emphasis on intergovernmental co-operation.

At the very least, Electronic Commerce provides governments with the opportunity to re-examine the established underpinnings of policies for trade and commerce. Many major kinds of strategic decisions about the national and international provision of network services now reside almost exclusively with the private sector. At the present time, many Electronic Commerce developments are occurring virtually outside the realm of government regulation.

Developments like these will have significant implications for the world economy in that they may dramatically modify the operation of markets and may have significant implications for employment and investment structures. Thus, they offer a challenge to governments to respond with new approaches to the governance of commercial activities that are flexible enough to achieve and preserve an appropriate balance between the interests of all social, political and economic constituencies at national and international levels.

As a first step, the Group believes that it is necessary to develop Policy Guidelines for those OECD Member countries that are pivotal to the emerging information economy. The adoption of such Guidelines would provide a reference point and an incentive for other countries to adopt similar approaches.

V.   Conclusions

The Group recognises that many of the issues discussed in this report have implications that apply in areas other than Electronic Commerce, and that policy discussions have been initiated already in a number of national and international frameworks. Our objective in preparing this document and in proposing recommendations, is to contribute to this dialogue by indicating some of the main policy priorities as perceived by companies that use electronic facilities extensively in their day-to-day business dealings with suppliers and customers.

Where substantive actions have already been initiated in the OECD and elsewhere to ensure that the information infrastructure is responsive to the needs of a wide range of commercial and non-commercial users, the Group broadly supports these actions. Where substantive actions are still required, the Group urges governments to formulate practical initiatives in consultation with users and producers of Electronic Commerce applications, and to pursue these initiatives vigorously, particularly to address legal issues arising in electronic commerce and to provide means of redress for those suffering from dishonest acts perpetrated in this environment.

Electronic Commerce is becoming established very quickly in all areas of the business world, and the Group believes strongly that the result will be imminent and dramatic changes, not only in the conduct of business, but in society and the economy at large. This is a view that emanates from the experience of our own firms, and those of the many firms and organisations that were consulted in the preparation of this report. We believe strongly that, as a source of social and economic opportunities, the Information Society presents governments with an urgent need to consult with the broadest range of participants – and particularly with corporate users and consumers.

Although the organisations we consulted had differing experiences with Electronic Commerce, and planned to pursue a diverse range of strategies, virtually all had come to the view that significant parts of their wealth-producing potential had already become, or would soon become, intertwined with their respective capabilities to operate in an Electronic Commerce environment. The removal of administrative and regulatory barriers to technological convergence and the provision of an open and easily accessible networking environment were seen to be key aspects of future competitiveness. Both government and industry will require maximum flexibility if they are to respond rapidly and productively to the rapidly evolving challenges of Electronic Commerce.

ANNEX A

Examples of Major Recent Governmental and Intergovernmental Actions to Promote Electronic Commerce

Government initiatives in supporting Electronic Commerce have been many and varied, and they are evolving all the time. While no claim is made that the following descriptions are comprehensive, or totally up-to-date, they are included to exemplify the kinds of Electronic Commerce initiatives that governments can elect to undertake.

G7

Following the 1995 G7 Ministerial Conference on the Global Information Society, the United States, Japan and the European Union accepted responsibility for the joint co-ordination of a project named "A Global Market Place for SMEs". "Theme One" of the project, co-ordinated by Japan, is concentrating on the global provision of business information to SMEs. "Theme Two", co-ordinated by the European Commission, is investigating SME requirements, including systems interoperability, security, privacy, legal issues, IPR, and electronic billing and payment systems. "Theme Three", co-ordinated by the United States, will involve establishing international Electronic Commerce test beds. The objective of the G7 project is to build bridges between existing national Electronic Commerce initiatives in order to promote an open Electronic Commerce environment conducive to the requirements of SMEs.

The United States

As the country with the highest volumes of data communication, the most network access and service providers, the most Internet hosts, and the highest total number of Internet connections, it is not surprising that the US government is taking a leading role in promoting Electronic Commerce. The National Information Infrastructure (NII) programme is a focal point of executive economic and social policy in the United States, and many projects of importance to Electronic Commerce are co-ordinated with the NII. Under an executive memorandum, the Federal Electronic Commerce Acquisition Team, including members from more than a dozen government agencies, was established in 1995 and charged with the task of defining an Electronic Commerce architecture for government use.

The "Team" is co-chaired by the General Services Administration (GSA), and the Department of Defense (DoD), and links a number of existing initiatives. The GSA, for example, is already engaged in the automation of the procurement system, including the tendering structure, and many other agencies have individual or linked initiatives related to Electronic Commerce. The DoD procurement requirements also included an extensive engineering, maintenance and logistics responsibility. Continuous Acquisition and Life-Cycle Support (CALS) is a DoD initiative that has already made some impact on private-sector organisational practices. The DoD is also involved with a US Post Office initiative to provide "trusted third-party" certification services for electronic transactions.

The Department of Commerce (DoC), through its National Institute for Standards and Technology (NIST), is involved in R&D for Electronic Commerce, and was instrumental in the development of the Digital Signature Standard (DSS). The Securities and Exchange Commission has automated the receipt, processing and distribution of all legally required filings of company documentation, and the Department of Veterans Affairs is developing an Electronic Commerce model for the delivery of Veterans benefits. The Internal Revenue Service has been expanding its "on-line" tax return facility since 1986, and in 1999 it will be mandatory for all US firms paying over US$20 000 in federal tax to file tax returns and make tax payments electronically.

Many private sector Electronic Commerce initiatives are linked to government projects either through co-funding or under the NII umbrella. Examples include the Electronic Messaging Association, Electronic Commerce Committee, the Enterprise Integration Network (EINet), the Electronic Manifest Bar Code (EMBARC), the Financial Services Technology Consortium (FSTC) and CommerceNet. Some of these, like CommerceNet, draw international participation.

The European Union

Since the early 1980s, the European Union has instituted a succession of programmes designed to develop trans-European networking capabilities. Most of these (ESPRIT, RACE, ACTS, etc.) have been R&D-oriented. There has also been European support for EDI systems, most notably the TEDIS (Trade EDI System) initiative. In 1994, at the request of the European Council, a group of prominent European ICT firms recommended specific actions in support of the development of a European information infrastructure.[29] Of the ten recommended target applications, four had direct relevance to Electronic Commerce – Telematic Services for SMEs, Electronic Tendering, Trans-European Public Administration Network and City Information Highways.

Since 1994, the European Commission has launched a formal "Electronic Commerce Initiative". In 1996, calls were issued under ESPRIT for R&D proposals from European firms specifically to support Electronic Commerce – including software, multimedia systems, high performance networking, integrated manufacturing and business process technologies.

Within the European Commission, primary responsibility for Electronic Commerce programmes is held by Directorate General III (Industry), and Directorate General XIII (Telecommunications, Information Market and Exploitation of Research). Most of the R&D programmes related to Electronic Commerce are administered by DG XIII. These include projects like SEMPER (Secure Electronic Market-place for Europe) an industry consortium co-funded by the EU under the ACTS Programme to develop an open and secure generic model covering the entire electronic trading cycle. DG III provided pilot funding for the BOLERO project on secure, paperless trading, and is now managing the IDA (Interchange of Data between Administrations) Programme aimed at enabling national and EU agencies to exchange administrative documentation in areas like healthcare, social security, procurement and customs. Other significant initiatives include SIMAP, an pan-European electronic procurement programme managed by DG XV (Internal Market and Financial Services), and the Commerce 2000 Programme, managed by DG XXIII (Enterprise Policy, Distributive Trades, Tourism and Co-operatives) aimed at encouraging Electronic Commerce in SMEs.

Japan

Japan is planning its Electronic Commerce strategies from a starting position that is the historical opposite to that of the United States. The penetration and usage rates of ICT in Japan are low by the standards of highly developed countries – for every computer per person in Japan, for example, there are roughly three computers per person in the United States. Moreover, although recent figures showed Japan to be second only to the United States in terms of installed computing "power" (measured in MIPS – "millions of instructions per second"), the US figure was seven times higher.[30]

Mindful of these discrepancies, in 1994 MITI began a major initiative to develop the Japanese "informatisation infrastructure", and MPT proposed a fibre-optic upgrade of the entire Japanese network by 2010. Soon afterwards, the Japanese Government announced a "five-year plan" to achieve full informatisation in government. By 1995, the government had issued a policy for "promoting an advanced information and telecommunications society", and embarked on a Programme for Advanced Industrial Information Infrastructure.

Against this background, the Electronic Commerce initiatives in Japan play very much on the already established strength and flexibility of Japanese industry. The Electronic Commerce Promotion Council (ECOM) is a recent initiative directed at developing both the technological and social infrastructures necessary to promote Electronic Commerce. About one-third of the roughly US$300 million ECOM budget is allocated to "consumer" Electronic Commerce and the rest to "corporate" Electronic Commerce. Principal ECOM projects include "virtual shopping mall" models, standards for product information, security, smart-card technologies, and authentication centres. The other major Japanese initiative concerns CALS, which Japanese interests are developing as a comprehensive manufacturing integration suite.

Australia

The development of Electronic Commerce is by no means restricted to very large economies. It should be remembered that of the top ten countries in terms of computer penetration per person, half of these countries (Norway, Finland, Denmark, Sweden and New Zealand) have populations of less than 10 million. With a population of about 17 million, Australia nevertheless ranks second in the world in terms of computer penetration and roughly eighth in the world in terms of installed computing power.

Australian government initiatives in Electronic Commerce are spread out between eight government agencies. The major current project is the co-ordination by the Department of Administrative Services of the migration to Electronic Commerce of all government procurement services. Electronic

Commerce migration is being supported by concurrent developments in the policy and legal structures, co-ordinated by the Attorney General's department, the Treasury, and the Taxation Office. Co-operating with industry, the Australian Government is co-funding the Tradegate organisation which is concerned with the introduction of electronic reporting procedures in the trade and transport chain. Under contract, Tradegate manages the electronic links between importing and exporting firms and the Australian Customs service.

ANNEX B

List of Firms and Organisations Contacted
and Interviewed in the Preparation of this Report

Company or Organisation	Person
Aamulehti Group	Matti Packalén
America Online	David Kirk
American Express	Allan Loren
American Petroleum Institute	Kendra Martin
	(Chair of ANSI/ASC/X12)
Andersen Consulting, Singapore	Willy Cheng
APACS	Chris Pearson
AT & T	Rohan Champion
BBN	
Bank of America	Marty Stein
Bank of England	Dean Blagdon
Bank of Finland	Raimo Hyvarinen
Bank of Montreal	Lloyd Darlington
Barclays Bank	Roger Alexander
Bertelsmann	Michael Behrens
Bass Brewers	Michael Fisher
Boeing	Walt W. Braithwaite
	Philip M. Lemoine
British Airways	Terry Butfield
Bull	M. Boule
Canadian Pacific Railroad	Anthony Foster
CCN	John Peace
Cebra (Toronto)	Renah Persofsky
CFK	Mark Kvamme
Citicorp	Jim Stojak
CommerceNet	Prof. Marty Tenenbaum
Commonwealth of Australia Government	Andy Macdonald (CIO)
Communications World (Delhi)	R. Giridhar

Compagnie Bancaire
Coryo – CM Life Ins. (Seoul)
Cybercash

Daimler Benz
DeTe Mobil
Deutsche Bahn
Deutsche Telekom
Direct Line
Disney
Dresdner Bank
EDB Singapore
EDI World Institute Toronto
EDS
EDventure Holdings
Electronic Commerce Association of Australia
Europay International
Federal Express
Five Paces Software
Ford
France Telecom
GIE Carte Bancaire
HP

IATA
IBM

ICL Retail
International Chamber of
Commerce (Paris)
Intuit
JCB
Karstadt
Kela/State Pension Fund
Kesko
Kleiner Perkins
Marks & Spencer
Mastercard International

Jean-Michel Billaut
John Ferguson
Ed Soo Hoo
Steve Crispinelli
Russell Stevenson
Dr. Lutz Eberhard
Roland Mahler
Dr. Ingo Brethamer
Bernard Bahn
Ian Chippendale
Dr. Sharon Garrett
Dr. Gunter Frank
Philip Yeo
Pierre Lortie
Hartmut Berger
Esther Dyson
Peter Blanchard
John Schey
Dennis Jones
Michael McChesney
Graham Gooding
Thierry Habert
Martine Briat
Dr. Joel Birnbaum
Dr. John Taylor
Mark Gasteen
Roger Hutt
Bruce Harreld
John Thompson
Kathy Kincaid
Horace Clemmons

Christiaan Van der Valk
Scott Cook
Atsushi Niimura
Carola Breker
Pentti Hoykinpuro
Paavo Tanskanen
Will Hearst
John Sacher
Gene Lockhart
Steve Mott

Merita Bank
Michelin
Microsoft

Nestlé
Netscape (Division Actra)
NatWest Retail Banking
News International
Nokia Mobile Phones
J C Penney
Peugeot Citroen

Precept Software
The Research Board

Rockwell
(Ex) Sabre
Security First Network Bank
Singapore Network Services
SITA
Skandia

Société Générale
Swift
Swiss DGD
Tidnings AB Marieberg
UK Government –
    Central IT Unit
    Customs & Excise
    Inland Revenue
UNCTAD
UNEC
Central Unit on IT
Unilever
US Government -
    Customs Service
    Dept. of Transportation
    Dept. of the Treasury
    GSA

Louis-Noel Jolly
Kalevi Kontinen
Philippe Tassin
Bill Gates
Bob Herbold
Jean Claude Dispaux
Jim Sha
Tim Jones
Richard Withey
Yrjo Neuvo
Dave Evans
Jean-Serge Bertoncini
Prof Alfred Piper
Judy Estrin
Naomi Seligman
Ernest von Simson
Jim Suter
Max Hopper
James Mohan III
Lim Keong
John Watson
Claes Oscarson
Ann-Christin G. Pehrsson
Alain Brodelle
Kailish Khanna
François Vuilleumier
Bengt Braun

Mark Gladwyn
Robin Maclachlan
Ian Spence
Bruno Lanvin
M. Hansell

James Duckworth

Dennis Sequeira
Bernestine Allen
Bernadette Curry
Martin Wagner

VISA (International)

Wal-Mart Stores
Zurich Insurance

Dick Lonergan
Carol Coye Benson
Linda Elliott
Randall Mott
Nicklaus Meyer

NOTES

1.   Figures from PFA Research, March 1995.

2.   S. Paltridge, "How Competition Helps the Internet," *OECD Observer*, No. 201, August/September 1996, pp. 25-28

3.   The figures are from ActivMedia, reported in *Business Week,* 23 September 1996.

4.   OECD, "Information Infrastructure Convergence and Pricing: The Internet" [OCDE/GD(96)73], Paris, p. 12.

5.   OECD, *op. cit.*, p. 24. The figures originated with CommerceNet/Nielsen.

6.   OECD/ISO, *The Economic Dimension of Electronic Data Interchange (EDI),* Geneva, 1996.

7.   K. Crowston and T. Malone, "Information Technology and Work Organisation," in T.J. Allen and M.S. Scott Morton (eds.) *Information and the Corporation of the 1990s,* Oxford, New York, 1994, pp. 249-275.

8.   This classification is adapted from R. Hawkins, J. Molas and W. Walker, "The Impact of CALS and CALS Principles on UK Industry Supply Chains", Report to the Department of Trade and Industry, February 1996.

9.   *Ibid.*

10.   OECD, *op. cit.*, p. 10.

11.   The figures were assembled by the Electronic Industries Association, Consumer Electronics Group, 1995.

12.   See OECD, Rapporteur's Report, Workshop No. 1 (Toronto) on the Economics of Information Societies, Paris, October 1995 [OCDE/GD(95)142]; and Rapporteur's Report, Workshop No. 2 (Istanbul) on the Economics of Information Societies, Paris, February 1996 [OCDE/GD(96)70].

13.   T.W. Malone, R.I. Benjamin and P. Yates, "Electronic Markets and Electronic Hierarchies", *Communications of the ACM*, Vol. 30, 1987, pp. 484-497.

14.   For perspectives on historical "lock-in" and path dependency, see Brian Arthur, "Competing Technologies, Increasing Returns, and Lock-In by Historical Events", *Economic Journal*, Vol. 99, March 1989, pp. 116-131; Paul David, "Clio and the Economics of QWERTY", *American Economic Review*, Vol. 75, No. 2, May 1985, pp. 332-337; and R. Mansell, "Designing Electronic Commerce," in R. Mansell and R. Silverstone, *Communication by Design: The Politics of Information and Communication Technologies*, Oxford University Press, Oxford, 1996, pp. 103-128.

15.   D.L Garcia, "Networking and the Rise of Electronic Commerce: The Challenge for Public Policy", *Business Economics*, Vol. 30, No. 4, October 1995, pp. 7-14.

16.   H.W. Chesbrough and D. Teece, "When is Virtual Virtuous?: Organising for Innovation," in *Harvard Business Review*, January/February 1996, pp. 65-73.

17.   J. Kokuryo and Y. Takeda, "The Role of Intermediaries in Electronic Commerce", paper presented at the OECD Workshop No. 2 on the Economics of Information Societies, Istanbul, Turkey, 14-15 December 1995.

18.   See G.N. von Tunzelmann, *Technology and Industrial Progress: The Foundations of Economic Growth*, Edward Elgar, Cheltenham, 1995.

19.   Financial Action Task Force on Money Laundering, *Report on Money Laundering Typologies*, OECD, Paris, February 1997.

20.   *Financial Times*, 19 November 1996, p. 6.

21.   Bank for International Settlements, *Implications for Central Banks of the Development of Electronic Money*, Basle, October 1996.

22.   For a more complete discussion of crytography in a policy context, refer to the OECD "Secretariat Report on Background and Issues of Cryptography Policy" (forthcoming).

23.   OECD, *Guidelines for the Security of Information Systems*, Paris, 1996.

24.   The OECD Recommendation of the Council Concerning Guidelines for Cryptography Policy was adopted on 27 March 1997 (publication forthcoming in 1997).

25.   OECD, *Guidelines on the Protection of Privacy and Transborder Flows of Personal Data*, Paris, 1981.

26.   The survey was conducted by International Data Corporation, and reported in *Communications Week International*, 4 March 1996, pp. 6-7.

27.   Paltridge, *op. cit.*

28.   OECD, "ICT Standardization in the New Global Context" [OCDE/GD(96)86], Paris.

29.   *Europe and the Global Information Society* (the "Bangemann Report"), Brussels, 26 May 1994.

30.   1994 figures from IMD, World Economic Forum.

MAIN SALES OUTLETS OF OECD PUBLICATIONS
PRINCIPAUX POINTS DE VENTE DES PUBLICATIONS DE L'OCDE

AUSTRALIA – AUSTRALIE
D.A. Information Services
648 Whitehorse Road, P.O.B 163
Mitcham, Victoria 3132   Tel. (03) 9210.7777
                              Fax: (03) 9210.7788

AUSTRIA – AUTRICHE
Gerold & Co.
Graben 31
Wien I   Tel. (0222) 533.50.14
                              Fax: (0222) 512.47.31.29

BELGIUM – BELGIQUE
Jean De Lannoy
Avenue du Roi, Koningslaan 202
B-1060 Bruxelles Tel. (02) 538.51.69/538.08.41
                              Fax: (02) 538.08.41

CANADA
Renouf Publishing Company Ltd.
5369 Canotek Road
Unit 1
Ottawa, Ont. K1J 9J3   Tel. (613) 745.2665
                              Fax: (613) 745.7660

Stores:
71 1/2 Sparks Street
Ottawa, Ont. K1P 5R1   Tel. (613) 238.8985
                              Fax: (613) 238.6041

12 Adelaide Street West
Toronto, QN M5H 1L6   Tel. (416) 363.3171
                              Fax: (416) 363.5963

Les Éditions La Liberté Inc.
3020 Chemin Sainte-Foy
Sainte-Foy, PQ G1X 3V6 Tel. (418) 658.3763
                              Fax: (418) 658.3763

Federal Publications Inc.
165 University Avenue, Suite 701
Toronto, ON M5H 3B8 Tel. (416) 860.1611
                              Fax: (416) 860.1608

Les Publications Fédérales
1185 Université
Montréal, QC H3B 3A7 Tel. (514) 954.1633
                              Fax: (514) 954.1635

CHINA – CHINE
Book Dept., China National Publiations
Import and Export Corporation (CNPIEC)
16 Gongti E. Road, Chaoyang District
Beijing 100020 Tel. (10) 6506-6688 Ext. 8402
                              (10) 6506-3101

CHINESE TAIPEI – TAIPEI CHINOIS
Good Faith Worldwide Int'l. Co. Ltd.
9th Floor, No. 118, Sec. 2
Chung Hsiao E. Road
Taipei   Tel. (02) 391.7396/391.7397
                              Fax: (02) 394.9176

**CZECH REPUBLIC –
RÉPUBLIQUE TCHÈQUE**
National Information Centre
NIS – prodejna
Konviktská 5
Praha 1 – 113 57   Tel. (02) 24.23.09.07
                              Fax: (02) 24.22.94.33
E-mail: nkposp@dec.niz.cz
Internet: http://www.nis.cz

DENMARK – DANEMARK
Munksgaard Book and Subscription Service
35, Nørre Søgade, P.O. Box 2148
DK-1016 København K   Tel. (33) 12.85.70
                              Fax: (33) 12.93.87

J. H. Schultz Information A/S,
Herstedvang 12,
DK – 2620 Albertslung   Tel. 43 63 23 00
                              Fax: 43 63 19 69
Internet: s-info@inet.uni-c.dk

EGYPT – ÉGYPTE
The Middle East Observer
41 Sherif Street
Cairo   Tel. (2) 392.6919
                              Fax: (2) 360.6804

FINLAND – FINLANDE
Akateeminen Kirjakauppa
Keskuskatu 1, P.O. Box 128
00100 Helsinki

Subscription Services/Agence d'abonnements :
P.O. Box 23
00100 Helsinki   Tel. (358) 9.121.4403
                              Fax: (358) 9.121.4450

*FRANCE
OECD/OCDE
Mail Orders/Commandes par correspondance :
2, rue André-Pascal
75775 Paris Cedex 16 Tel. 33 (0)1.45.24.82.00
                          Fax: 33 (0)1.49.10.42.76
                          Telex: 640048 OCDE
Internet: Compte.PUBSINQ@oecd.org

Orders via Minitel, France only/
Commandes par Minitel, France
exclusivement : 36 15 OCDE

OECD Bookshop/Librairie de l'OCDE :
33, rue Octave-Feuillet
75016 Paris   Tel. 33 (0)1.45.24.81.81
                               33 (0)1.45.24.81.67

Dawson
B.P. 40
91121 Palaiseau Cedex   Tel. 01.89.10.47.00
                          Fax: 01.64.54.83.26

Documentation Française
29, quai Voltaire
75007 Paris   Tel. 01.40.15.70.00

Economica
49, rue Héricart
75015 Paris   Tel. 01.45.78.12.92
                          Fax: 01.45.75.05.67

Gibert Jeune (Droit-Économie)
6, place Saint-Michel
75006 Paris   Tel. 01.43.25.91.19

Librairie du Commerce International
10, avenue d'Iéna
75016 Paris   Tel. 01.40.73.34.60

Librairie Dunod
Université Paris-Dauphine
Place du Maréchal-de-Lattre-de-Tassigny
75016 Paris   Tel. 01.44.05.40.13

Librairie Lavoisier
11, rue Lavoisier
75008 Paris   Tel. 01.42.65.39.95

Librairie des Sciences Politiques
30, rue Saint-Guillaume
75007 Paris   Tel. 01.45.48.36.02

P.U.F.
49, boulevard Saint-Michel
75005 Paris   Tel. 01.43.25.83.40

Librairie de l'Université
12a, rue Nazareth
13100 Aix-en-Provence   Tel. 04.42.26.18.08

Documentation Française
165, rue Garibaldi
69003 Lyon   Tel. 04.78.63.32.23

Librairie Decitre
29, place Bellecour
69002 Lyon   Tel. 04.72.40.54.54

Librairie Sauramps
Le Triangle
34967 Montpellier Cedex 2 Tel. 04.67.58.85.15
                          Fax: 04.67.58.27.36

A la Sorbonne Actual
23, rue de l'Hôtel-des-Postes
06000 Nice   Tel. 04.93.13.77.75
                          Fax: 04.93.80.75.69

GERMANY – ALLEMAGNE
OECD Bonn Centre
August-Bebel-Allee 6
D-53175 Bonn   Tel. (0228) 959.120
                          Fax: (0228) 959.12.17

GREECE – GRÈCE
Librairie Kauffmann
Stadiou 28
10564 Athens   Tel. (01) 32.55.321
                          Fax: (01) 32.30.320

HONG-KONG
Swindon Book Co. Ltd.
Astoria Bldg. 3F
34 Ashley Road, Tsimshatsui
Kowloon, Hong Kong   Tel. 2376.2062
                          Fax: 2376.0685

HUNGARY – HONGRIE
Euro Info Service
Margitsziget, Európa Ház
1138 Budapest   Tel. (1) 111.60.61
                          Fax: (1) 302.50.35
E-mail: euroinfo@mail.matav.hu
Internet: http://www.euroinfo.hu//index.html

ICELAND – ISLANDE
Mál og Menning
Laugavegi 18, Pósthólf 392
121 Reykjavik   Tel. (1) 552.4240
                          Fax: (1) 562.3523

INDIA – INDE
Oxford Book and Stationery Co.
Scindia House
New Delhi 110001   Tel. (11) 331.5896/5308
                          Fax: (11) 332.2639
E-mail: oxford.publ@axcess.net.in

17 Park Street
Calcutta 700016   Tel. 240832

INDONESIA – INDONÉSIE
Pdii-Lipi
P.O. Box 4298
Jakarta 12042   Tel. (21) 573.34.67
                          Fax: (21) 573.34.67

IRELAND – IRLANDE
Government Supplies Agency
Publications Section
4/5 Harcourt Road
Dublin 2   Tel. 661.31.11
                          Fax: 475.27.60

ISRAEL ISRAËL
Praedicta
5 Shatner Street
P.O. Box 34030
Jerusalem 91430   Tel. (2) 652.84.90/1/2
                          Fax: (2) 652.84.93

R.O.Y. International
P.O. Box 13056
Tel Aviv 61130   Tel. (3) 546 1423
                          Fax: (3) 546 1442
E-mail: royil@netvision.net.il

Palestinian Authority/Middle East:
INDEX Information Services
P.O.B. 19502
Jerusalem   Tel. (2) 627.16.34
                          Fax: (2) 627.12.19

ITALY – ITALIE
Libreria Commissionaria Sansoni
Via Duca di Calabria, 1/1
50125 Firenze   Tel. (055) 64.54.15
                          Fax: (055) 64.12.57
E-mail: licosa@ftbcc.it

Via Bartolini 29
20155 Milano   Tel. (02) 36.50.83

Editrice e Libreria Herder
Piazza Montecitorio 120
00186 Roma   Tel. 679.46.28
                          Fax: 678.47.51

Libreria Hoepli
Via Hoepli 5
20121 Milano   Tel. (02) 86.54.46
                      Fax: (02) 805.28.86

Libreria Scientifica
Dott. Lucio de Biasio 'Aeiou'
Via Coronelli, 6
20146 Milano   Tel. (02) 48.95.45.52
                      Fax: (02) 48.95.45.48

JAPAN – JAPON
OECD Tokyo Centre
Landic Akasaka Building
2-3-4 Akasaka, Minato-ku
Tokyo 107   Tel. (81.3) 3586.2016
                      Fax: (81.3) 3584.7929

KOREA – CORÉE
Kyobo Book Centre Co. Ltd.
P.O. Box 1658, Kwang Hwa Moon
Seoul   Tel. 730.78.91
                      Fax: 735.00.30

MALAYSIA – MALAISIE
University of Malaya Bookshop
University of Malaya
P.O. Box 1127, Jalan Pantai Baru
59700 Kuala Lumpur
Malaysia   Tel. 756.5000/756.5425
                      Fax: 756.3246

MEXICO – MEXIQUE
OECD Mexico Centre
Edificio INFOTEC
Av. San Fernando no. 37
Col. Toriello Guerra
Tlalpan C.P. 14050
Mexico D.F.   Tel. (525) 528.10.38
                      Fax: (525) 606.13.07
E-mail: ocde@rtn.net.mx

NETHERLANDS – PAYS-BAS
SDU Uitgeverij Plantijnstraat
Externe Fondsen
Postbus 20014
2500 EA's-Gravenhage Tel. (070) 37.89.880
Voor bestellingen: Fax: (070) 34.75.778

Subscription Agency/Agence d'abonnements :
SWETS & ZEITLINGER BV
Heereweg 347B
P.O. Box 830
2160 SZ Lisse   Tel. 252.435.111
                      Fax: 252.415.888

NEW ZEALAND –
NOUVELLE-ZÉLANDE
GPLegislation Services
P.O. Box 12418
Thorndon, Wellington Tel. (04) 496.5655
                      Fax: (04) 496.5698

NORWAY – NORVÈGE
NIC INFO A/S
Ostensjoveien 18
P.O. Box 6512 Etterstad
0606 Oslo   Tel. (22) 97.45.00
                      Fax: (22) 97.45.45

PAKISTAN
Mirza Book Agency
65 Shahrah Quaid-E-Azam
Lahore 54000   Tel. (42) 735.36.01
                      Fax: (42) 576.37.14

PHILIPPINE – PHILIPPINES
International Booksource Center Inc.
Rm 179/920 Cityland 10 Condo Tower 2
HV dela Costa Ext cor Valero St.
Makati Metro Manila   Tel. (632) 817 9676
                      Fax: (632) 817 1741

POLAND – POLOGNE
Ars Polona
00-950 Warszawa
Krakowskie Prezdmiescie 7 Tel. (22) 264760
                           Fax: (22) 265334

PORTUGAL
Livraria Portugal
Rua do Carmo 70-74
Apart. 2681
1200 Lisboa   Tel. (01) 347.49.82/5
                      Fax: (01) 347.02.64

SINGAPORE – SINGAPOUR
Ashgate Publishing
Asia Pacific Pte. Ltd
Golden Wheel Building, 04-03
41, Kallang Pudding Road
Singapore 349316   Tel. 741.5166
                      Fax: 742.9356

SPAIN – ESPAGNE
Mundi-Prensa Libros S.A.
Castelló 37, Apartado 1223
Madrid 28001   Tel. (91) 431.33.99
                      Fax: (91) 575.39.98
E-mail: mundiprensa@tsai.es
Internet: http://www.mundiprensa.es

Mundi-Prensa Barcelona
Consell de Cent No. 391
08009 – Barcelona   Tel. (93) 488.34.92
                      Fax: (93) 487.76.59

Libreria de la Generalitat
Palau Moja
Rambla dels Estudis, 118
08002 – Barcelona
                  (Suscripciones) Tel. (93) 318.80.12
                  (Publicaciones) Tel. (93) 302.67.23
                      Fax: (93) 412.18.54

SRI LANKA
Centre for Policy Research
c/o Colombo Agencies Ltd.
No. 300-304, Galle Road
Colombo 3   Tel. (1) 574240, 573551-2
                  Fax: (1) 575394, 510711

SWEDEN – SUÈDE
CE Fritzes AB
S–106 47 Stockholm   Tel. (08) 690.90.90
                      Fax: (08) 20.50.21

For electronic publications only/
Publications électroniques seulement
STATISTICS SWEDEN
Informationsservice
S-115 81 Stockholm   Tel. 8 783 5066
                      Fax: 8 783 4045

Subscription Agency/Agence d'abonnements :
Wennergren-Williams Info AB
P.O. Box 1305
171 25 Solna   Tel. (08) 705.97.50
                      Fax: (08) 27.00.71

Liber distribution
Internatinal organizations
Fagerstagatan 21
S-163 52 Spanga

SWITZERLAND – SUISSE
Maditec S.A. (Books and Periodicals/Livres
et périodiques)
Chemin des Palettes 4
Case postale 266
1020 Renens VD 1   Tel. (021) 635.08.65
                      Fax: (021) 635.07.80

Librairie Payot S.A.
4, place Pépinet
CP 3212
1002 Lausanne   Tel. (021) 320.25.11
                      Fax: (021) 320.25.14

Librairie Unilivres
6, rue de Candolle
1205 Genève   Tel. (022) 320.26.23
                      Fax: (022) 329.73.18

Subscription Agency/Agence d'abonnements :
Dynapresse Marketing S.A.
38, avenue Vibert
1227 Carouge   Tel. (022) 308.08.70
                      Fax: (022) 308.07.99

See also – Voir aussi :
OECD Bonn Centre
August-Bebel-Allee 6
D-53175 Bonn (Germany) Tel. (0228) 959.120
                       Fax: (0228) 959.12.17

THAILAND – THAÏLANDE
Suksit Siam Co. Ltd.
113, 115 Fuang Nakhon Rd.
Opp. Wat Rajbopith
Bangkok 10200   Tel. (662) 225.9531/2
                      Fax: (662) 222.5188

TRINIDAD & TOBAGO, CARIBBEAN
TRINITÉ-ET-TOBAGO, CARAÏBES
Systematics Studies Limited
9 Watts Street
Curepe
Trinidad & Tobago, W.I. Tel. (1809) 645.3475
                        Fax: (1809) 662.5654
E-mail: tobe@trinidad.net

TUNISIA – TUNISIE
Grande Librairie Spécialisée
Fendri Ali
Avenue Haffouz Imm El-Intilaka
Bloc B 1 Sfax 3000   Tel. (216-4) 296 855
                      Fax: (216-4) 298.270

TURKEY – TURQUIE
Kültür Yayinlari Is-Türk Ltd.
Atatürk Bulvari No. 191/Kat 13
06684 Kavaklidere/Ankara
                  Tel. (312) 428.11.40 Ext. 2458
                  Fax : (312) 417.24.90

Dolmabahce Cad. No. 29
Besiktas/Istanbul   Tel. (212) 260 7188

UNITED KINGDOM – ROYAUME-UNI
The Stationery Office Ltd.
Postal orders only:
P.O. Box 276, London SW8 5DT
Gen. enquiries   Tel. (171) 873 0011
                      Fax: (171) 873 8463

The Stationery Office Ltd.
Postal orders only:
49 High Holborn, London WC1V 6HB
Branches at: Belfast, Birmingham, Bristol,
Edinburgh, Manchester

UNITED STATES – ÉTATS-UNIS
OECD Washington Center
2001 L Street N.W., Suite 650
Washington, D.C. 20036-4922
                      Tel. (202) 785.6323
                      Fax: (202) 785.0350
Internet: washcont@oecd.org

Subscriptions to OECD periodicals may also
be placed through main subscription agencies.

Les abonnements aux publications périodiques
de l'OCDE peuvent être souscrits auprès des
principales agences d'abonnement.

Orders and inquiries from countries where Distributors have not yet been appointed should be
sent to: OECD Publications, 2, rue André-Pascal, 75775 Paris Cedex 16, France.

Les commandes provenant de pays où l'OCDE
n'a pas encore désigné de distributeur peuvent
être adressées aux Éditions de l'OCDE, 2, rue
André-Pascal, 75775 Paris Cedex 16, France.

12-1996

CITY OF WESTMINSTER
RECEIVED ON

2 5 JUN 1997

WESTMINSTER REFERENCE LIBRARY